Editor

Stephanie Buehler, Psy.D.

Managing Editor

Ina Massler Levin, M.A.

Editor-in-Chief

Sharon Coan, M.S. Ed.

Illustrator

Sue Fullam

Cover Artist

Denice Adorno

Product Manager

Phil Garcia

Imaging

Rosa C. See

Publishers

Rachelle Cracchiolo, M.S. Ed.
Mary Dupuy Smith, M.S. Ed.

Using the Six-Trait Writing Model

Six Traits of Writing
- Idea and Content
- Word Choice
- Fluency
- Voice
- Organization
- Convention

WESTERN EDUCATIONAL ACTIVITIES LTD.
12006 - 111 Ave. Edmonton, Alberta T5G 0E6
Ph: (780) 413-7055   Fax: (780) 413-7056
GST # R105636187

Author

Tracie Heskett

Teacher Created Materials, Inc.

6421 Industry Way
Westminster, CA 92683
www.teachercreated.com

©2001 Teacher Cr_____ ____ _____ Inc.

Reprir____

ISBN-0-

Mad___

Table of Contents

Six Traits for Instruction and Assessment

What Is Six-Trait Writing?

In the early 1980s, teachers in the northwestern United States felt they needed a set of common guidelines by which to teach and assess student writing. By comparing student writing needing extensive revision to student writing that did not, certain characteristics, or traits, emerged. The qualities found in successful student writing have been revised over time to form what is now known as "Six-Trait Writing." Northwest Regional Educational Laboratories in Portland, Oregon, has been instrumental in defining and developing the six traits and making workshops and other resources available to teachers.

The six analytic traits identified for use in instructing and assessing student writing are as follows:

- Ideas and Content
- Voice
- Word Choice
- Organization
- Fluency
- Conventions

(For a definition of each trait, refer to the corresponding first page of each section in this book.)

Why Should I Teach Six-Trait Writing?

The Six-Trait Model allows teachers and students to focus on one element of writing at a time, thus breaking the task of learning to write effectively into manageable parts.

Current academic standards refer to these qualities specifically (i.e., voice, word choice, and conventions). The six traits apply to a variety of writing styles and purposes. Mastery of these traits goes beyond simply "teaching to the test" and gives students skills they can use for life.

How Do I Teach Six-Trait Writing in the Classroom?

One trait can be taught each week for six weeks; there are five daily lessons for each of the six traits. A teacher may also teach one entire trait on a single day as a more comprehensive thematic unit. Lessons should be taught in the order given as many lessons build on material previously covered and/or exercises already completed. Have students write in a writing notebook or save their writing in a folder for future use.

When completing the writing exercises, students should skip a line in their writing or double space; these rough drafts will be used in later lessons to provide editing practice.

Since older students seem to like having permission to read and enjoy picture books, the literature-based lessons for each trait are based upon them; each literature-based lesson also provides suggested chapter books to be used, if desired.

Each lesson incorporates one or more academic standards. These standards are from *Content Knowledge: A Compendium of Standards and Benchmarks for K–12 Education* (Second Edition, 1997) synthesized by John S. Kendall and Robert J. Marzano. The book is published jointly by McREL (Mid-continent Regional Educational Laboratory, Inc.) and ASCD (Association for Supervision and Curriculum Development). Used by permission of McREL. Other standards addressed but not specifically identified include reading, communication, and presentation.

Standards for Writing
Grades 3-5

1. Demonstrates competence in the general skills and strategies of the writing process

A. Prewriting: Uses prewriting strategies to plan written work (e.g., uses graphic organizers, story maps, and webs; groups related ideas; takes notes; brainstorms ideas)

B. Drafting and Revising: Uses strategies to draft and revise written work (e.g., elaborates on a central idea; writes with attention to voice, audience, word choice, tone, and imagery; uses paragraphs to develop separate ideas)

C. Editing and Publishing: Uses strategies to edit and publish written work (e.g., edits for grammar, punctuation, capitalization, and spelling at a developmentally-appropriate level; considers page format [paragraphs, margins, indentations, titles]; selects presentation format; incorporates photos, illustrations, charts, and graphs)

D. Evaluates own and others' writing (e.g., identifies the best features of a piece of writing, determines how own writing achieves its purposes; asks for feedback; responds to classmates' writing)

E. Writes stories or essays that show awareness of intended audience

F. Writes stories or essays that convey an intended purpose (e.g., to record ideas, to describe, to explain)

G. Writes expository compositions (e.g., identifies and stays on the topic; develops the topic with simple facts, details, examples, and explanations; excludes extraneous and inappropriate information)

H. Writes narrative accounts (e.g., engages the reader by establishing a context and otherwise creates an organizational structure that balances and unifies all narrative aspects of the story; uses sensory details and concrete language to develop plot and character; uses a range of strategies such as dialogue and tension or suspense)

I. Writes autobiographical compositions (e.g., provides a context within which the incident occurs; uses simple narrative strategies; provides some insight into why this incident is memorable)

Standards for Writing
Grades 3-5 *(cont.)*

J. Writes expressive compositions (e.g., expresses ideas, reflections, and observations; uses an individual, authentic voice; uses narrative strategies, relevant details, and ideas that enable the reader to imagine the world of the event or experience)

K. Writes in response to literature (e.g., advances judgements; supports judgements with references to the text, other works, other authors, non-print media, and personal knowledge)

L. Writes personal letters (e.g., includes the date, address, greeting, and closing; addresses envelopes)

---

2. Demonstrates competence in the stylistic and rhetorical aspects of writing

A. Uses descriptive language that clarifies and enhances ideas (e.g., describes familiar people, places, or objects)

B. Uses paragraph form in writing (e.g., indents the first word of a paragraph; uses topic sentences; recognizes a paragraph as a group of sentences about one main idea; writes several related paragraphs)

C. Uses a variety of sentence structures

---

3. Uses grammatical and mechanical conventions in written compositions

A. Writes in cursive, types, or uses word processing

B. Uses exclamatory and imperative sentences in written compositions

C. Uses pronouns in written compositions (e.g., substitutes pronouns for nouns)

D. Uses nouns in written compositions (e.g., uses plural and singular naming words; forms regular and irregular plurals of nouns; uses common and proper nouns; uses nouns as subjects)

E. Uses verbs in written compositions (e.g., uses a wide variety of action verbs, past and present verb tenses, simple tenses, forms of regular verbs; verbs agree with subjects)

F. Uses adjectives (e.g., indefinite, numerical, predicate adjectives) in written compositions

G. Uses adverbs in written compositions (e.g., to make comparisons)

H. Uses coordinating conjunctions in written compositions (e.g., links ideas using connecting words)

I. Uses negatives in written compositions (e.g., avoids double negatives)

Standards for Writing
Grades 3-5 *(cont.)*

J. Uses conventions of spelling in written compositions (e.g., spells high-frequency, commonly misspelled words from appropriate grade-level list; uses a dictionary and other resources to spell words; uses initial consonant substitution to spell related words; uses vowel combinations for correct spelling)

K. Uses conventions of capitalization in written compositions (e.g., titles of people; proper nouns [names of towns, cities, counties, and states; days of the week; months of the year; names of streets; names of countries; holidays]; first word of direct quotations; heading, salutation, and closing of a letter)

L. Uses conventions of punctuation in written compositions (e.g., uses periods after imperative sentences and in initials, abbreviations, and titles before names; uses commas in dates and addresses and after greetings and closings in a letter; uses apostrophes in contractions and possessive nouns; uses quotation marks around titles and with direct quotations; uses a colon between hours and minutes)

4. Gathers and uses information for research purposes

A. Uses a variety of strategies to identify topics to investigate (e.g., brainstorms, lists questions, uses idea webs)

B. Uses encyclopedias to gather information for research topics

C. Uses dictionaries to gather information for research topics

D. Uses key words, indexes, cross-references, and letters on volumes to find information for research topics

E. Uses multiple representations of information (e.g., maps, charts, photos) to find information for research topics

F. Uses graphic organizers (e.g., notes, charts, graphs) to gather and record information for research topics

G. Compiles information into written reports or summaries

Character Pattern for Classroom Display

Teacher Directions: Many lessons require a poster display of a specific figure. Enlarge and reproduce the pattern six times and decorate them as follows: scientist, police officer, juggling clown, teacher, hiking guide, and mechanic. You will find directions for their use in the initial lessons on each trait.

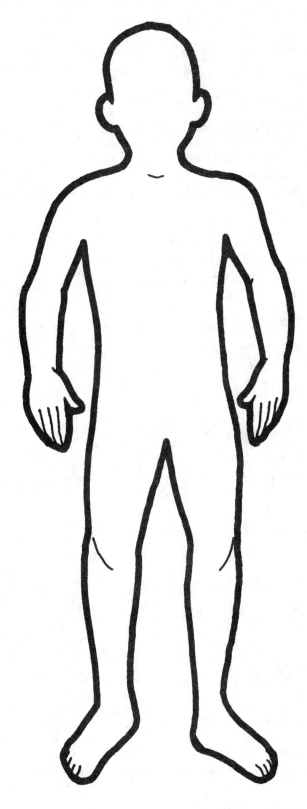

Ideas and Content Trait

The Ideas and Content Trait helps students gather and organize their ideas in order to use them more efficiently. Students learn to use what they know and to present their ideas clearly to the reader. In the lessons that follow, the characteristics of this trait are taught metaphorically using scientists and the scientific process as they apply to writing.

Think about the role and tasks of the scientist, then think how these relate to the role and tasks of the writer. A scientist is an expert, or specialist, in a given field. A scientist investigates and explores, conducts research, and seeks knowledge. The scientific process includes formulating a hypothesis based on previous knowledge, gathering data, and modifying the hypothesis to accommodate new information. Everything is relevant—there is nothing useless in a lab experiment.

Likewise, a writer investigates and explores a topic. A writer must collect ideas, or data, about the topic and present them in a novel way that adds to a reader's body of knowledge about that topic. Clear writing, rooted in the author's experience, shows insight and understanding and will convince the reader to keep reading. Like an experiment, a well-written piece leads the reader to a convincing conclusion. In good writing, as in the lab, nothing is extraneous. Good writing comes from adequate preparation and organization of ideas—and that is the core of the Ideas and Content Trait.

Introducing the Scientist

Objective

Given a definition of a scientist, the student will identify characteristics of the Ideas and Content Trait by writing them on a poster for display.

Standards

- Standard 4: Gathers and uses information for research purposes
- Standard 4A: Uses a variety of strategies to identify topics to investigate
- Standard 4C: Uses dictionaries to gather information for research topics
- Standard 4G: Compiles information into written reports or summaries

Materials

- Lab coat and other scientific apparatus (optional)
- Character pattern for classroom display (page 7), dressed as a scientist
- Dictionary, thesaurus, or other reference material

Lesson Opening

Wearing the lab coat, ask students what a scientist does. Talk about a scientist's job to generate a hypothesis or idea based on knowledge; generate data; and reach and present a conclusion. Talk about how this relates to the writer's job of finding a topic, generating ideas, and writing in a way that leads to a satisfying conclusion.

Lesson Directions

1. Introduce the job of scientist and relate it to the characteristics of the Ideas and Content Trait. Teach the specific characteristics of the trait, using overhead, board, or other teaching aids. Tell students that their writing will have strong ideas and content when they do the following:
   - Generate an intriguing topic
   - Connect their writing to prior experience
   - Use relevant, specific details
   - Have clear ideas
   - Surprise the reader with what they know

2. Have the class brainstorm characteristics of a scientist. Students should then look up the definition of scientist in the dictionary or other reference material. (A scientist is an expert, specialist, investigator, laboratory technician, explorer, research worker, serious student, seeker of knowledge, etc.) Discuss how a scientist's job is similar to that of a writer. Ask students to draw a scientist and fill in characteristics of the Ideas and Content Trait around their figure.

3. Have volunteers copy definitions from their individual papers to the scientist character pattern for classroom display.

Lesson Closing

Ask students, "How do scientists help us? How will this trait help us in our writing? What do you think the hardest thing will be for you as you try to put this trait into practice in your own writing? What will be the easiest thing to remember?"

Monsters in My Backyard

Objective

After a review of the Ideas and Content Trait and a read-aloud experience, students will use qualities of this trait when writing about a family event.

Standards

- Standard 1I: Writes autobiographical compositions (e.g., provides a context within which the incident occurs; uses simple narrative strategies; provides some insight into why this incident is memorable)

Materials

- Picture book: *Where the Wild Things Are* by Maurice Sendak. HarperCollins, 1963.
- Chapter book options: *Harry Potter* by J. K. Rowling. Scholastic, 1997. *A Wrinkle in Time* by Madelaine L'Engle. Farrar, Straus and Giroux, 1962.
- Monster Patterns (page 11), one for each student
- Craft sticks (optional)
- Crayons or markers

Lesson Opening

Ask students the following questions: "Do you have any relatives who say or do unique things? How do you react to them? Think of a time in your family when something unusual happened just because one person acted in a certain way."

Lesson Directions

1. If you are using the picture book option, read *Where the Wild Things Are* aloud to the class.

2. Discuss with students how the author incorporated qualities of the Ideas and Content Trait in his writing. For example, Sendak connects his writing to his own experience (in interviews, Sendak has spoken about the fact that his stories are based on childhood events), uses specific details, shows rather than tells, and develops the story.

3. Demonstrate the fact that every element of writing should add something to the whole. Do this by selecting sentences or passages of the book and asking students what would happen if the sentences or passages were removed.

4. If using the chapter book option, discuss the plot. How has the author incorporated qualities from the Ideas and Content Trait in his or her writing?

5. Have students write about a specific event that has occurred in their families. If the class needs a specific idea to prompt their thinking, display the following story starter:

   When [a relative] came to visit, [an event that happened].

6. Ask for volunteers to share their stories with partners, in small groups, or with the entire class.

7. As an extension, use the monster patterns on page 11. Have students make puppets and write or tell stories about their monsters.

Lesson Closing

"You've heard stories from one or more of your classmates. Why are qualities from the Ideas and Content Trait useful when writing stories? What happens if the author does not follow these guidelines (for example, he or she includes details that are not relevant or fails to keep the reader in mind)?"

Monster Patterns

Directions: Color the monsters below and glue them to either craft sticks to make puppets or onto paper. Tell a partner a story about scary monsters. Write your story on separate paper.

The Makings of an Experiment

Objective

Given a graphic organizer, the student will write his or her ideas to use in developing content in writing.

Standards

- Standard 1A: Uses prewriting strategies to plan written work (e.g., uses graphic organizers, groups related ideas, takes notes, brainstorms ideas)
- Standard 1B: Uses strategies to draft and revise written work (e.g., elaborates on a central idea, uses paragraphs to develop separate ideas)
- Standard 1G: Writes expository compositions (e.g., identifies and stays on the topic; develops the topic with simple facts, details, examples, and explanations; excludes extraneous and inappropriate information)

Materials

- Any science apparatus available to the teacher (beakers, test tubes, gloves, small Bunsen burners, etc.)
- Creating Topics (page 13), one for each student
- My Ideas (page 14), one for each student

Lesson Opening

Ask the class the following question: "What is the first thing a scientist does before conducting an experiment? (Collect materials and tools.) In the same way, gathering ideas helps a writer develop the content of his or her writing."

Lesson Directions

1. Distribute page 13 and introduce the concept of brainstorming. Ask students to brainstorm for a set time period (e.g., two minutes).
2. Review characteristics of the Ideas and Content Trait using the scientist poster.
3. Distribute page 14. Have students choose one topic from page 13 to expand in detail. Students will fill in areas of the work sheet with relevant details, experiences, knowledge, and examples.
4. Give students about ten minutes to write a paragraph or two expanding on their idea, experience, or example from page 14.

Lesson Closing

Say to students, "Now you have generated some data with which to begin to write. What ideas did you generate that excite you enough to write about?" Tell students to keep these pages in their writing note-books as they will use them in a day or two to develop some writing content.

Extension Activity

If time allows, tell students they now have all the data they need to write a story. Have them draw on their experience to form a plot. Remind them to include their relevant details and to use their background knowledge/examples to help them develop the story and make it believable to the reader. Model some sample writing on the board or overhead using an example/experience from your own life, if necessary.

Creating Topics

Directions: Use this page to brainstorm topics of interest to you. The pictures scattered on the page can help you get started.

_____

_____

_____

_____

_____

_____

_____

_____

_____

_____

_____

_____

_____

_____

_____

_____

_____

_____

_____

_____

_____

_____

My Ideas

Directions: Use this page to organize your ideas about one of your topics from page 13.

Examples

What You Know

Topic

Experiences

Details

Scientific Evidence

Objective

Given verbal prompts, the student will construct a story map of his or her life to date.

Standards

- Standard 1A: Uses prewriting strategies to plan written work (e.g., uses story maps, groups related ideas)
- Standard 1I: Writes autobiographical compositions (e.g., provides a context within which the incident occurs; uses simple narrative strategies; provides some insight into why this incident is memorable)

Materials

- Large sheets of drawing paper
- Colored pencils or colored markers

Lesson Opening

Ask students to think back to the first lesson. Say, "We've been talking about scientists, how they work and how that relates to developing your own ideas and content in your writing. Before conducting an experiment, do scientists base their hypotheses on something previously known? Why?" Use the questions as a springboard to review the scientific process as it relates to writing.

Lesson Directions

1. Have students draw a line—straight, curved, whatever shape they want—to represent their life to date.

2. Go through landmarks for the map one at a time, having students use a different color pencil or marker for each one. Consider asking students to create an icon or symbol for each event.

   - Main events (birth, start of school, etc.)
   - When special people came into your life or crossed your path (friends, teachers, coaches)
   - Times when something bad happened
   - Good times, special events (special holidays, vacations, etc.)

3. Choose an event—from your own story map or a student's—and do a shared writing exercise to illustrate constructing a story from what you know.

4. Ask students to share with a partner one experience from their story maps about which they could write.

5. Explain "free writing" rules: keep writing, stay silent, stop editing. Then direct students to write a short story about one thing from their story map. Give them 10–15 minutes of free writing time to get started, then allow them to continue on their own.

6. Collect and save the story maps for use with My Voice (page 41).

Lesson Closing

Call on two or three students to surprise the class with what they know. Ask how they could build upon this experience as a scientist to construct a story.

What Do Your Senses Tell You?

Objective

Given things to see, touch, hear, smell, and taste, the student will write about his or her observations using clear writing in such a way as to show, rather than tell, the reader of his or her experience.

Standards

- Standard 1F: Writes stories or essays that convey an intended purpose (e.g., to describe, to explain)
- Standard 1J: Writes expressive compositions (e.g., expresses ideas, reflections, and observations; uses an individual, authentic voice; uses relevant details; and presents ideas that enable a reader to imagine the world, the event or experience)

Materials

- Objects to look at, touch, and smell (cotton balls, shells, flower petals, spices, etc.) for three centers
- Upbeat cassette or CD of instrumental music for listening center
- Small snack (e.g., mini-marshmallows, chocolate chips, raisins) placed into paper cups for taste center
- Blank word cards and pencils for imagination center

Preparation

Set up the six centers, one for each of the five senses, plus the sixth sense of imagination. Be sure to check for food allergies or to get parent permission before passing out any food.

Lesson Opening

Remind students that scientists experiment by observing data and recording their findings, stating, "Today, you will have the opportunity to be 'scientific' authors."

Lesson Directions

1. Review characteristics of the trait. Ask students what is meant by "show, don't tell."

2. Ask students to name the five senses and what they do. (They give us information about the world around us.) How can this help in our writing? (The use of sensory information helps writers to focus on a topic and use specific details.) Discuss with class the concept of a sixth sense, that of imagination.

3. Divide class into six groups and send one group to each center to experience using one of their senses. The imagination center group will receive "imagination" word cards; each student will write about the word on his or her card.

4. When the students have experienced each center, have them do one of the following exercises:
   - Write about their favorite sensory experiences and why this is so
   - Write one sentence about each sensory experience
   - Write a paragraph telling how sensory information helps us be better writers

Lesson Closing

Once more, relate the scientific process of gathering data and generating ideas to the writing process. Remind students that just as scientists must present their conclusions in an article, writers must present their work in a logically written piece of work.

Word Choice Trait

Words. Words are everywhere. What makes some words more effective than others? What makes one word a better choice than another word? Strong, visual words help an author present an image to his or her reader. It is important to find just the right word to convey the intended meaning, to use words that are accurate and precise. Action verbs and words with energy keep a story moving. The words an author chooses to use need not be long or fancy; it can be equally important to use words that sound natural yet specific.

The way an author uses words can make a difference in how interesting a piece of writing is to read. Writers create pictures with words, and using words in new ways can expand the perspective of both the author and the reader. The sound of words, whether read silently or aloud, adds to the meaning as well.

The first two lessons in this section focus on identifying effective words. In the remaining lessons, students are encouraged to use words to describe things in new and different ways. Students will begin to compile a list of their favorite words; this list can become a resource for them to use in subsequent lessons and activities.

Using Vibrant Words

Objective

Given the basic characteristics of the Word Choice Trait, the student will compile lists of words that make writing more interesting, as well as words that do not fit the trait of word choice, and put these words in the appropriate places on a poster(s).

Standards

- Standard 1A: Uses prewriting strategies to plan written work (e.g., uses story maps, groups related ideas)

Materials

- Two large sheets of poster board
- Word cards and tape
- Character pattern for classroom display (page 7)
- Police-related items, e.g., cap, badge, whistle

Preparation

Decorate one sheet of poster board to look like a jail cell. Decorate the other sheet as a "free zone." Enlarge and decorate the character pattern as a police officer.

Lesson Opening

Wear one or more police-related items. Direct students' attention to the "jail" poster displayed in room. Tell students they will be sending words to jail today.

Lesson Directions

1. Teach the students that effective word choice means using the following:
   - Words that evoke strong visual imagery
   - Words that are accurate and precise
   - Action verbs that give writing energy
   - Words that sound natural
   - Words that evoke sound

2. Explain that some words are too general or overused in student writing. Ask students to write such words on cards to place on word jail poster.

3. Ask students to brainstorm a list of words that fit the positive qualities of this trait (see list of sample words below). Have students record words in their notebooks; they will keep their own word lists for later use. You might also want them to write some words on cards and place visually opposite the jail poster in the free zone.

Sample words

- Amused
- Barley
- Beckon
- Carbon
- Cliff
- Dare
- Flimsy
- Gypsy
- Hailstones
- Petrified
- Raven
- Seize
- Shatter
- Splashed
- Sneak
- Tease
- Thunder
- Translucent

Lesson Closing

Review qualities of the Word Choice Trait, with student input. Call on students one at a time to fill in a characteristic of word choice on the police officer poster.

Staying Out of Word Jail

Objective

Given a selection from literature, the students become aware of how an author uses word choice by identifying words that do or do not meet the criteria of the Word Choice Trait.

Standards

- Standard 1D: Evaluates others' writing (e.g., identifies the best features of a piece of writing, specifically related to word choice)
- Standard 1K: Writes in response to literature (e.g., advances judgements; supports judgements with references to the text, characteristics of the Word Choice Trait, and personal knowledge)

Materials

- Picture book: *Stellaluna* by Janell Cannon. Scholastic, 1993.
- Chapter book option: *Island of the Blue Dolphins* by Scott O'Dell. Houghton Mifflin, 1960.
- Jail and free zone posters (see page 18)
- Word cards

Preparation

Print vivid words from *Stellaluna* or *Island of the Blue Dolphins* on the word cards and display them on the free zone poster.

Lesson Opening

Show students the word cards you added to the free zone poster from the selected piece of literature. Ask students what makes these words stand out.

Lesson Directions

1. Review characteristics of the Word Choice Trait.

2. Read the poetry samples (page 20). Point out examples of words or word phrases that add to the visual imagery: red-checked, sneaked, sound bursts, crowded, flit, flashing, dance, held captive.

3. Read the picture book aloud, or, if using the chapter book, have students silently read a selected passage, sharing books if necessary.

4. Have students identify words in the literature that do or do not have characteristics of strong word choice. If reading the picture book, give students cards to write words on as they listen to the story. Students will then place their cards on the appropriate posters. If using a passage from a chapter book, have students make a list of words that have those qualities that add interest to the writing as they read. These words may then be written on cards and displayed as suggested above.

Lesson Closing

Ask students if they learned any new words they would like to add to their notebooks. Which characteristics of the Word Choice Trait do these words have?

Extension Activity

Have students write their own poetry using words from the word lists in their notebooks.

Staying Out of Word Jail *(cont.)*

Sample Poetry

Mexican Feast

We all got there in time for dinner—
red-checked tablecloth
and candles
(one without a wick).
We sneaked
tortilla chips and
olives to put on fingers.
The more, the noisier—
sound bursts forth as
we delight
in having the front room
to ourselves,
grownups crowded in the kitchen.
At last,
A moment of silence
for thanks.
Olé!

—Tracie Heskett

Water Dance

They flit about the rocks
Fairy sprites
in bathing trunks
red, green, orange, blue flashing
through the stillness
I marvel at the silence
as they dance in
a magical world
of water skippers,
bugs under stones,
held captive by a somber gray-green
lagoon.
They
pose
ready for flight.

—Tracie Heskett

Words, Words, Everywhere

Objective

Given index cards and a class-generated list of words, the student will label classroom objects in a novel way to expand his or her perspective.

Standards

- Standard 1A: Uses prewriting strategies to plan written work (e.g., uses story maps, groups related ideas)
- Standard 2A: Uses descriptive language that clarifies and enhances ideas (e.g., describes familiar places or objects)
- Standard 3D: Develops awareness of nouns and uses them in writing
- Standard 3E: Develops awareness of verbs and uses them in writing
- Standard 3F: Develops awareness of adjectives and uses them in writing

Materials

- Index cards, two to three per student
- Objects to label (optional)
- Four sheets of chart paper or tagboard
- *poemcrazy* by Susan G. Woolbridge. Clarkson Potter, 1996. (teacher's reference, optional)

Preparation

Label each sheet of chart paper or tagboard as follows: Nouns, Verbs, Adjectives, Other

Lesson Opening

Ask students, "What are some of your favorite words? Why? What do you like about these words?"

Lesson Directions

1. Write some student-volunteered favorite words on the board.
2. Read some word samples (*poemcrazy*, pages 12–13, 16 and 18).
3. Display labeled word charts. Begin discussion by referring to the student-generated list on the board. Ask students on which chart to put their favorite words. Have the class brainstorm more words to add to the charts. Use words from the lists provided to stimulate their thinking, if necessary.
4. Introduce concept of "word tickets" (*poemcrazy*, pages 14–18). Explain to students that they will write words on index cards (one word per card, two to three cards per student). Do not tell students their next task until they have written their words.
5. Have students use the cards to label objects around the room. Cards may be propped up next to the object or taped to it (e.g., to the door). Emphasize that the labels will not make sense! For example, they may end up with a tapered door, a juicy window, a galloping chalkboard, etc.
6. Once students have finished, you may walk around the room and read the labeled objects to them. Or, you may want students to discover labeled objects for themselves.
7. Ask students if the labels change the way they see these things.

Lesson Closing

Ask students, "What are words good for? What are we going to do with all these words?" (Enjoy them, use them in writing; put word charts in same area of room as the "free zone" set up in an earlier lesson.)

Word Collage

Objective

Given many words to choose from, the student will create a collage that expresses a specific idea or concept.

Standards

- Standard 1J: Writes expressive composition (e.g., expresses ideas, reflections, and observations; uses an individual, authentic voice; uses relevant details; and presents ideas that enable a reader to imagine the world of the event or experience)

Materials

- Old magazines with language appropriate for classroom use and/or newspapers
- 9" x 12" (23 cm x 30 cm) construction paper, one per student, or a large piece of tagboard, one per group
- Glue

Lesson Opening

Ask students, "What does this quote say to you: 'A picture is worth a thousand words'? Have you ever heard of a 'word picture'? What is it?"

Lesson Directions

1. Review characteristics of the Word Choice Trait.

2. Explain and discuss the concept of *word collage*. A word collage contains words that communicate thoughts and feelings to another person. Share the sample word collage below with your students. Ask them to guess the concept (a friend helping a friend).

3. Encourage students to think of an idea or concept (e.g., peace, rest, family, conflict, etc.) that they would like to express using words. Then introduce the activity of cutting words from magazines and gluing them on the construction paper to make a word collage.

4. Ask students to write a story based on their own word collages. Students can share their collages and stories with the class.

Lesson Closing

Select students at random to share their collages. Have the class first guess what idea they think is being portrayed in the collage; next, have students read specific words and describe why these words were included. Ask students what makes these words effective. (Refer to word choice characteristics poster during discussion, if necessary.)

The World's Greatest Product

Objective

Given words that the class has collected during the previous lessons, as well as from other supplemental resources, the student will create a product and then write an advertisement for it.

Standards

- Standard 1F: Writes stories or essays that convey an intended purpose (e.g., to record ideas, to describe, to explain)

Materials

- Word charts and lists from student notebooks
- Dictionaries, thesauruses, and other "word" resource materials (optional)
- Sample advertisements and/or product descriptions
- The World's Greatest Product (page 24), one copy for each student

Lesson Opening

Ask students, "What product would you like to develop? How would you tell someone about your new product or describe it so they would want to buy it?"

Lesson Directions

1. Discuss the Word Choice Trait, particularly as it relates to writing product descriptions (e.g., precise word use, action verbs, high energy language, how words sound, etc.).

2. Display sample advertisements and descriptions on overhead, chart, or board; or distribute them among students if there are enough samples.

3. Identify words meeting criteria of the Word Choice Trait. Note their use, if applicable (e.g., action words).

4. Distribute page 24. Have students work with partners to invent a product using this graphic organizer. Students should fill in each box on the work sheet as it pertains to their product. Remind students to use specific and descriptive words that have qualities of strong word choice.

5. Select as many partners as time allows for reading their descriptions to the class. Ask students if they can tell what product is being described by the partners' advertisement. Would they want to buy this product? Why or why not?

Lesson Closing

Have students identify specific words used that were effective. Add the words to one of the class word lists.

The World's Greatest Product *(cont.)*

Name of your product

_____

What does your product look like?

_____

_____

_____

_____

What does it do?

_____

_____

_____

_____

How is your product special or different from others?

_____

_____

_____

How will it benefit the buyer?

_____

_____

_____

Why should someone buy this?

_____

_____

_____

How much does it cost?
How can the buyer pay for it?

_____

_____

_____

How can someone order your product?

_____

_____

Illustration of your product:

Fluency Trait

The opening lesson in this section metaphorically uses a juggling clown to familiarize students with the Fluency Trait. We think of a clown as someone who plays. Clowns also often match the mood around them. As a juggler, a clown has an excellent sense of rhythm; he or she never misses a beat. A juggling clown's actions flow together smoothly, with movements flowing from one to another. Everything he or she does has a purpose. Likewise, words are the writer's props; a writer juggles words, manipulates them, plays with them. The writer conveys a mood not only by the words he or she chooses, but also by using language, rhythm, and sentence structure.

Fluent writing has many of these same characteristics. The author plays with the language, using word patterns and rhythm to convey his message to the reader. Fluent writing incorporates natural rhythm and flow. It passes the read aloud test. The fluent author uses clear sentences that make sense, with no extra words. Sentence length and structure are varied; ideas begin purposefully and connect with each other.

Students begin this series of lessons by playing and having some fun with juggling, while reviewing the characteristics of the trait. They are then encouraged to engage in a process of thinking, playing a game of "What if . . . ?" You may opt to have the class continue to play with rhythm and word patterns by reading aloud a picture book to younger students. Students continue to build their sense of rhythm and natural flow by writing while listening to music. In the fourth lesson, students break out of the mold by writing mixed-up silly stories. In the final lesson, they bring it all back together again by writing a complete story from start to finish, using as many qualities of the Fluency Trait as possible.

Juggling for Fluency

Objective

Given rubber balls, the student will review the characteristics of fluency by interacting with a partner and other class members.

Standards

- Standard 2: Develops awareness of stylistic and rhetorical aspects of writing (i.e., sentence structure and rhythm)

Materials

- Character pattern for classroom display (page 7)
- Colored rubber balls
- Circles cut from colored paper
- Juggling Clown (page 27)
- Clown attire to be worn by teacher, if so inclined

Preparation

Enlarge and decorate the character pattern to appear as a juggling clown. Make one overhead copy of page 27. Reproduce one copy of page 27 for each student.

Lesson Opening

Ask the students, "When you think of someone who likes to play with rhythm and patterns, all the while reflecting different moods, of whom do you think? Perhaps you think of a street musician or a clown—someone who can sing, dance, juggle, and pantomime others."

Lesson Directions

1. Teach the trait by presenting its characteristics (below). As each characteristic is presented, write it on the transparency of the clown figure. Tell students the following about writing fluently:
   - Varies sentence length and structure
   - Has natural rhythm and flow
   - Uses a process of thinking (e.g., asks the question, "What if . . . ?")
   - Uses different word patterns
   - Plays with language
   - Has clear sentences that make sense
   - Has ideas that begin purposefully and connect to one another
   - Matches the mood
   - Has no extra words
   - Passes the read-aloud test

2. Group students in pairs, two colored balls to each pair. Have students toss balls back and forth, reviewing and naming a characteristic of the trait each time.

3. Turn off overhead, if you haven't already done so. Distribute page 27 and have students fill in the juggling balls with trait characteristics by recalling class discussion without aid of the overhead.

Lesson Closing

Ask volunteers to name a quality, write it on a colored paper circle, and add it to the clown character pattern for classroom display.

Juggling Clown

Directions: Write characteristics of fluent writing in each of the clown's juggling balls.

What If . . . ?

Objective

Given a read-aloud experience with literature, the student will experiment with word patterns and language by writing his or her own story.

Standards

- Standard 1K: Writes in response to literature
- Standard 2A: Uses descriptive language that clarifies and enhances ideas (e.g., describes familiar people, places, or objects)
- Standard 2B: Uses paragraph form in writing (e.g., uses topic sentences)
- Standard 2C: Uses a variety of sentence structures

Materials

- Picture book: *Sam and the Tigers* by Julius Lester. Dial Books for Young Readers, 1996.
- Chapter book option: *Hatchet* by Gary Paulsen. Simon and Schuster, 1987.
- What If . . . ? (page 29), one copy for each student
- Props for reading buddies (optional)
- Word cards

Preparation

Write one characteristic of fluent writing on each word card.

Lesson Opening

Say to students, "Yesterday, we talked about rhythm and word patterns. Will we only find these traits in music or poetry? Why or why not?"

Lesson Directions

1. Go over characteristics of fluency with students, stressing word patterns, natural rhythm (achieved by varied sentence length), and play with language.

2. Display the word cards. Ask students to listen for the elements of fluency as you read the story *Sam and the Tigers* aloud to the class.

3. Distribute page 29 and introduce the "What If . . . ?" ideas for stories and poetry. Then have students write for a set period, perhaps 15–20 minutes. Encourage them to focus on qualities listed on the word cards as they write.

4. If using the chapter book option, select at least two passages from the book that you feel illustrate fluent writing. Distribute a copy of the book to each pair of students. Have them read a selected passage aloud to a partner. Switch readers after 5–10 minutes; they may finish reading the passage or read another selection. Continue as in Step 3 above.

Lesson Closing

Tell students to think about the story *Sam and the Tigers* or *Hatchet*. What elements of fluency did they hear? In what ways did the author use rhythm, a variety of sentence structures, word patterns, and play with language to tell a story?

Arrange with another class of younger students to have your students read and present *Sam and the Tigers*. Have students work on rhythm and play with language as they practice reading. Divide the class into groups and have each group take one section of the book.

Story Ideas Based on *Sam and the Tigers*

- What if you were walking through the jungle and ran into a tiger? or two? or three?
- What if Sam had met different animals other than tigers?
- What if your clothes were as brightly colored as Sam's clothes? How would you describe them? Would they be as red as . . . , yellow as . . . , purple as . . . , or silver as . . . , etc.)
- What if your mother fixed pancakes for dinner? What is your favorite way to eat pancakes? What is your favorite breakfast food to have for dinner?

Story Ideas Based on *Hatchet*

- What if you were in a plane that crashed in the wilderness?
- What if Brian's plane had crashed somewhere else (e.g., not by a lake)?
- What would you do if you were in Brian's situation?
- What if Brian had not been rescued?
- What if you were attacked by a moose? or something else?
- What if you had to find something to eat in the woods? Would it be funny? or difficult?

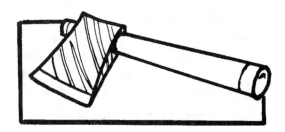

Poetry Ideas

- Write a rhyming poem.
- Write a poem describing an adventure.
- Write a poem describing colors.
- Write a list poem.
- Write a funny poem.
- Write a poem that plays with language and words.
- Condense the story of *Sam and the Tigers* or *Hatchet* into a poem.

The Music of Language

Objective

Given music to listen to, the student will write for a specified period of time, then check his or her paper for rhythms.

Standards

- Standard 1J: Writes expressive composition (e.g., expresses ideas, reflections, and observations; uses an individual, authentic voice; uses relevant details; and presents ideas that enable a reader to imagine the world of the event or experience)
- Standard 2A: Uses descriptive language that clarifies and enhances ideas
- Standard 2B: Uses paragraph form in writing
- Standard 2C: Uses a variety of sentence structures

Materials

- Percussion instruments and objects students could use to beat out a rhythm, e.g., dowels or spoons
- Instrumental music tape or CD and player

Lesson Opening

Beat out a rhythm on the percussion instruments or objects. Ask students to copy the rhythm with their hands on their desks. Talk about rhythm. Ask students, "Does human talking sound like music? Why or why not? What do talking and music have in common?"

Lesson Directions

1. Review the characteristics of the Fluency Trait.
2. Review the rules of free writing: keep writing, stay silent, work without editing.
3. Play the instrumental tape. Have students write for 10 minutes while music plays.
4. When time is up, have students get with a partner. One student will read his or her paper, and the partner will beat out any rhythm that is in the sound of the words. Switch roles.

Lesson Closing

Ask students if they found it easy or hard to write to music. Did this exercise help them to put "natural rhythm and voice flow" into their writing? When they read their paper to their partner, did the writing have more of a sense of rhythm than usual?

Silly Stories

Objective

Given a "story starter," the student will develop a sense of continuity in writing as he or she creates a story by taking turns adding to the writing or telling.

Standards

- Standard 1D: Evaluates others' writing (e.g., identifies the best features of a piece of writing, determines how own writing achieves its purposes, asks for feedback, responds to classmates' writing)
- Standard 1H: Writes narrative accounts (e.g., engages the reader by establishing a context and otherwise developing reader interest; establishes a situation, plot, point of view, setting, and conflict; uses sensory details and concrete language to develop plot and character; uses a range of strategies such as dialogue and tension or suspense)

Materials

- Character pattern (page 7) of clown on classroom display
- Colored markers or overhead pens
- Silly Stories (page 32)

Preparation

Reproduce one copy of page 32 for each student. Draw a basic figure outline on the overhead or chalkboard to decorate as a clown during the lesson.

Lesson Opening

As motivation, draw the students' attention to the figure on the overhead or chalkboard and solicit items and colors of clothing from them, adding each one as it is mentioned. When the drawing is finished, ask students what this person they "dressed" looks like. Relate discussion to the clown character pattern in your classroom display that was completed in the Juggling for Fluency lesson.

Lesson Directions

1. Review characteristics of the Fluency Trait.

2. Place students into small groups of five. Give each student a different story starter.

3. Have students write two sentences of their story. Students then pass their paper to the next person in the group, who will add two more sentences. Have students continue in this manner until together they have written five silly stories.

4. Select students at random to read their "silly" story to the class. Ask the class to comment on the stories.

Lesson Closing

Ask students how these stories do or do not demonstrate qualities of fluency. Why or why not? What factors affected the fluency? Did this make the stories harder or easier to read and understand?

Silly Stories *(cont.)*

Teacher Directions: Make enough copies so that each student within each group has a different story starter. See page 31.

Story Starter #1

Katie lay in bed staring at the water stain right over her head on the ceiling. It was shaped like a key, and she often imagined it was a map of a different country . . .

Story Starter #2

"Look!" Jake pointed a finger at the light flickering through the trees beyond the cabin window. Colin didn't answer. Instead, he covered his head with his sleeping bag . . .

Story Starter #3

Once upon a time, there was a princess who lived in a castle by the sea. She could not speak, but everyone enjoyed her sweet smile and kind deeds . . .

Story Starter #4

"I'm running away and never coming back!" Reagan stomped her feet and ran outside. She slammed the door behind her . . .

Story Starter #5

Silently, I walked up to the edge of the crowd. The people were intent, watching some activity in the middle of the courtyard. I stood on my toes and tried to see over the heads of those standing in front of me . . .

Write Your Own Script

Objective

Given pictorial and written prompts, the student will create a story in written form.

Standards

- Standard 1A: Uses prewriting strategies to plan written work (e.g., uses graphic organizers, groups related ideas, takes notes, brainstorms ideas)
- Standard 1B: Uses strategies to draft and revise written work (e.g., elaborates on a central idea, uses paragraphs to develop separate ideas)
- Standard 1H: Writes narrative accounts (e.g., engages the reader by establishing a context and otherwise developing reader interest; establishes a situation, plot, point of view, setting, and conflict; uses sensory details and concrete language to develop plot and character; uses a range of strategies such as dialogue and tension or suspense)

Materials

- Five large sheets of tagboard
- Magazines and other resource materials for photos (see Preparation, below)
- 4" x 6" (10 cm x 15 cm) index cards, five for each student
- Clown character pattern on classroom display

Preparation

Label the tagboard sheets as follows: Character, Setting of Place, Setting of Time, Mood, and Conflict. Find magazine photos or use words to make a visual display illustrating the heading on each sheet of tag board. Use these posters to designate stations around the classroom.

Lesson Opening

Welcome students to the "[name of class or school] Theater." Explain that the theater's script writers have become ill or detained and that the producer must have a script. Tell students they are to provide the missing story.

Lesson Directions

1. Remind students that script writers have guidelines to follow. Direct their attention to the fluency characteristics displayed. These are their "guidelines" for the day's assignment.
2. Divide class into five groups and distribute five index cards to each student. Ask students to label the cards as follows: Characters, Setting of Place, Setting of Time, Mood, and Conflict. Direct students to rotate through the stations designated by the posters, using the posters as springboards for ideas that they are to write on the appropriate index card. Allow students 2–3 minutes at each station.
3. After each group has visited all five stations, have students return to their seats and write a short script using the notes on their index cards.
4. Allow students to give brief performances of their scripts and congratulate them for producing work for the theater on such short notice.

Lesson Closing

Ask students to think back to the previous day's "silly stories." Which stories were easier, more natural, to read? Why? Which aspects of fluency were easy for students to incorporate into their stories? Which were harder to use?

Voice Trait

Recall the voices of your teachers. Did they all use the same language and style to convey knowledge? Each teacher's style reflects his or her voice; a personality comes through in teaching. In a similar way, each writer also has a voice, or a unique way of expressing him or herself. Writing that has strong voice is sincere, honest, focused on the audience, while at the same time reflecting the author's own personality. The reader can sense a real person behind the words.

To develop a unique voice, an author must know him- or herself as a writer and then write out of that knowledge. Writers develop their voice by writing with confidence and bringing the topic to life. Just as a teacher may focus on the individual, writers write to the reader. A writer who uses strong voice will be himself/herself without trying to exaggerate or impress the reader. The writing will come from the author's thoughts, feelings, and who he or she is as a person.

Students will begin learning about voice by practicing to be teachers; by doing so, they will discover that every person in the class has his or her own unique voice. They will then practice identifying voice as a given author has used this trait in his or her writing. Students also are asked to read work by anonymous authors and try to guess what kind of person wrote the piece. The final two lessons in this section allow students to develop their own voice by drawing on their own experiences and writing a personal letter to a friend.

The Teacher's Voice

Objective

Given the characteristics of the trait, the student will teach a characteristic of voice to his or her classmates.

Standards

- Standard 1A: Uses prewriting strategies to plan written work (e.g., uses graphic organizers, groups related ideas, takes notes, brainstorms ideas)
- Standard 2: Develops awareness of stylistic and rhetorical aspects of writing, specifically related to voice
- Standard 4: Gathers and uses information for research purposes
- Standard 4A: Uses a variety of strategies to identify topics to investigate (e.g., brainstorms)
- Standard 4G: Compiles information into reports or summaries, specifically to present orally to classmates

Materials

- Overhead or white board and markers
- Character pattern for classroom display (page 7)

Preparation

Reproduce and enlarge page 7 and decorate it as a teacher.

Lesson Opening

Ask students to think about teachers they have had over the years. How are they different from one another? Discuss how each teacher has his or her style of teaching, a unique personality or voice.

Lesson Directions

1. Teach the trait. Talk about the characteristics of the Voice Trait using examples from your own teaching experience, if possible. Share with the students that voice . . .

   - makes a piece sound like a particular person wrote it
   - allows the author's personality to come through the writing
   - has natural rhythm
   - hooks the reader, calling attention to the writing
   - conveys honesty and requires self-knowledge
   - writes to the reader
   - brings the topic to life
   - gives writing personality, letting the reader sense a real person behind the words
   - talks directly to the reader

2. Have students work with a partner. Assign each pair one characteristic of the Voice Trait to teach to the rest of the class. In their lesson, they should state the trait, tell what it means in their own words, and give an example.

3. When students have completed writing the lesson, direct students to present them. They may use a white board, overhead, or any notes they wrote as partners to teach. Remind students to show respect and good listening skills for fellow classmates.

What Is the Character Saying?

Objective

After a read-aloud experience, the student will write pieces of dialogue as they might be spoken by different characters.

Standards

- Standard 1K: Writes in response to literature (e.g., advances judgements; supports judgements with references to the text, characteristics of the word choice trait, and personal knowledge)

Materials

- Picture book: *More Than Anything Else* by Marie Bradby. Orchard Books, 1995.
- Chapter book option: *Thunder Cave* by Roland Smith. Hyperion Books for Children, 1995. (Use one book per four students.)
- What Is the Character Saying? (page 37)

Preparation

Reproduce one copy of page 37 for each student.

Lesson Opening

Ask students, "Have you ever read stories where it feels like the author talks directly to you? What makes it seem that way?"

Lesson Directions

1. Guide students in reviewing characteristics of voice as the class discusses any books in which it seems the author is speaking directly to the reader.

2. Read the book *More Than Anything Else* aloud to the class. Discuss how the author's and characters' voices come through in the writing.

3. Distribute page 37. Have students create four characters, either real or pretend or a combination. What would the character talk about? What language would the character use? What words would the character say? Then, students can write the characters' words in a conversation bubble. The students can then label the character on the line below, e.g., a young teacher on the first day on the job.

4. Select students to read the characters' words from their papers and allow their classmates to try to guess what type of person is speaking.

Lesson Closing

Say to students, "In the story we read today, did it sound like a real person was telling the story? Why or why not? What did he or she say that made it feel like he or she was talking to you, the reader, directly? What are some ways you could begin to use the qualities of this trait in your own writing?"

What Is the Character Saying? *(cont.)*

Directions: Think of a character. What would the character say? What would the character talk about? Write the character's words in a conversation balloon. Then label the character.

Who Is Talking?

Objective

Given writing samples, the student will identify strong voice by answering specific questions. Given a description of a fictional character, the student will write in the "person's" voice.

Standards

- Standard 1D: Evaluates own and others' writing (e.g., identifies the best features of a piece of writing, determines how own writing achieves its purposes, asks for feedback, responds to classmates' writing)
- Standard 1J: Writes expressive composition (e.g., expresses ideas, reflections, and observations; uses an individual, authentic voice; uses relevant details; and presents ideas that enable a reader to imagine the world of the event or experience)

Materials

- Who Is Talking? (pages 39–40)
- Sample stamped envelope and letter addressed to you at school

Preparation

Copy pages 39–40 onto either one transparency or onto five separate transparencies so that you can display the sample letters to students one at a time.

Lesson Opening

Ask students if they are able to tell who wrote the letter to you just by seeing the envelope. Might they be able to identify the author if they read it?

Lesson Directions

1. Review the characteristics of the voice trait.

2. Show one overhead or one letter at a time from pages 39–40. Ask the students questions about each piece of writing:

    - Who do you think wrote this?
    - Who is talking here? Is it a male or female? How old is the person?
    - What might this person's job be?
    - Does the writing sound like a real person talking?

3. List specific characters on the board, e.g., a 17-year-old football player, an 80-year-old book seller, etc. Have students write a letter to the class in the voice of one character.

Lesson Closing

Read two or three student paragraphs aloud anonymously. Ask the class if they can match the paragraph to a character on the board, and if so, which one. Does it sound like that "person" wrote it? or did the student's own voice come through?

Who Is Talking? *(cont.)*

Teacher Directions: Copy this page and the following onto overheads, or make a separate overhead for each paragraph (see page 38).

Sample Paragraph #1

I like to begin walks on the bridge at One Mile. There's always action here in the park near my house. Water rushes over the dam. Trout and trout shadows dart about the still spots. In summer, there's a sweet, creek, sycamore smell.

Today it's early September and oak galls are dropping—the puffy golf-sized balls oak trees form around wasp larvae. A blackened gall spins on a step of the dam below the bridge. The gall bobs under the tiny falls and hops back up in a circle like a science class experiment nobody's watching but me.

Sample Paragraph #2

I am bidding you goodbye now, my friend. Surely my days on this Earth are of even fewer count than I had figured.

Last night I got home from work; put on my new orange helmet; wheeled my screaming-orange, 21-speed, rapid-fire shifting mountain bike out of the garage; and prepared to ride to the local fire station to license the creature.

A brief break in traffic afforded me the chance to pedal across semi-busy Wilson Street. I stood on the pedal and pulled on the handlebars for momentum and—boom!—my feet kicked out from under me and my chest hit the bars. I flopped down in the middle 'turning lane' of Wilson with cars coming from both directions! When I recovered my senses, I saw my one pedal lying back at the driveway entrance to the apartments. I gathered the parts and limped back to my own abode, where I discovered that the bike shop had not screwed in my pedals!

Who Is Talking? *(cont.)*

Sample Paragraph #3

We now have a cement slab for the new house next door west to us. I suspect tomorrow will be the day they begin putting up the sides and rafters. It has been interesting to watch all the steps from our kitchen window. Last Friday when the slab was poured, it took at least eight fellows, maybe more.

Sample Paragraph #4

I feel violence is a problem because of the effect it has on ordinary people. I don't understand how people can be so ignorant, how they can do such mean things to other people. It is scary when you hear on the news how somebody has killed seven people, or . . . There should be harsh punishments for such things. Sometimes I think the death penalty is not even enough.

Sample Paragraph #5

So, how's it going? Were you a little scared on the first day of school? I was a little bit curious but not really scared. My border on my name tag was really terrific. I just wish the teacher had spelled my name right. But what can you expect with a name like Flingenbocher? I wish I had a name like yours, Hill.

My Voice

Objective

Given prompts, the student will consider aspects of his or her life that can provide material for his or her writing by adding to previously begun story maps.

Standards

- Standard 1A: Uses prewriting strategies to plan written work (e.g., uses graphic organizers, groups related ideas, takes notes, brainstorms ideas)
- Standard 1I: Writes autobiographical compositions (e.g., provides a context within which the incident occurs, uses simple narrative strategies, provides some insight into why this incident is memorable.)
- Standard 1J: Writes expressive compositions (e.g., expresses ideas, reflections, and observations; uses an individual, authentic voice; uses relevant details; and presents ideas that enable a reader to imagine the world of the event or experience)

Materials

- Student story maps from Scientific Evidence (see page 15)
- Colored pencils
- Character pattern of teacher on classroom display

Lesson Opening

Ask students, "Who are you? When do you feel the most like you?" Call the class to silence for a few moments while they reflect on their answers. (Students may need to be reminded not to look at each other, make faces or gestures, or laugh.)

Lesson Directions

1. Have students take out their story maps from previous lesson.
2. Review and discuss characteristics of the Voice Trait, using the class poster or other visual aids if necessary.
3. Refer back to the time of silence at beginning of the lesson. Ask students how they felt and what they thought of when they heard the opening questions.
4. Direct students to use a color not yet used on their story map and mark times and/or events when they were able to rest or relax, be themselves, and have fun.
5. Have students also mark (using the same or different colors) times when they felt most like themselves, and note the circumstances surrounding those times.
6. Next, students will mark times when something sad happened, as well as what they learned from the experience, and/or how they were able to help someone else out of that experience.
7. Have students write a paragraph or two about something from their life in their own voice.
8. Instruct students not to put their name on their papers. Collect all the papers and redistribute them to the class. Have students try to guess whose papers they have based on voice. If many of the students know their classmates' handwriting, have them put their names on their papers and turn them in. Type the paragraphs, leaving the names off, enlisting volunteer help if available.

Lesson Closing

Ask students if it was easy or difficult to recognize a classmate's writing by what they had written, without having a name on the paper. Why or why not? What characteristics of voice did the author use that helped you, the reader, understand the "voice?"

Signed, Me

Objective

Given an example of a personal letter displaying the characteristics of voice, the student will compose a letter to a friend or relative and mail it.

Standards

- Standard 1E: Writes stories or essays that show awareness of intended audience
- Standard 1L: Writes personal letters (e.g., includes the date, address, greeting, and closing; addresses envelopes)

Materials

- Paper for rough drafts (optional)
- Stationery for final drafts (if available, use computer-generated stationery and offer a few different designs for students to choose from)
- Stamps
- Envelopes
- Personal letter or e-mail (one you personally have received)

Lesson Opening

Say to students, "We all like to get mail. What is the best part about reading a letter?"

Lesson Directions

1. Read selections from a personal letter that demonstrates qualities of the Voice Trait. Ask students to identify those characteristics exemplified in the letter you just read.

2. Discuss how students might use characteristics of the Voice Trait in their own letter writing (e.g., being yourself, not trying to exaggerate or impress your reader, writing out of your own thoughts, feelings, and who you are, bringing your topic to life, etc.)

3. Have students think of a real person to whom they would like to write. Remind them to use the qualities just discussed as they write. Depending on your class, you might want them to write a rough draft first before they write a final copy on stationery. This will also allow the teacher to check student writing for voice.

4. Have students write a final copy of their letter on stationery and prepare it for mailing. Students should address their own envelopes; younger students might need a review of the form for addressing envelopes.

5. Collect letters for mailing. (See if parents will volunteer postage or if there is money for postage from the parent-teacher organization.)

Lesson Closing

Ask students if they felt using the characteristics of the Voice Trait make their letter easier and more interesting to read and write. Why? Would they like to receive such a letter? Why or why not?

Organization Trait

This section uses hiking as a metaphor for organizing writing. The trait of organization gives the reader a clear path through a written work. Writers are guides, leading the reader through the story. Writing with the quality of organization has a clear direction and will not lose the reader. Transitions tie together and there is appropriate pacing throughout the writing; it flows smoothly. Just as a guide makes sure everyone is together at the beginning of a hike and leads them to a satisfactory conclusion at the end, a writer grabs the reader's attention and provides a satisfying conclusion that makes the reader think.

Like a trail map, a graphic organizer is a tool to help authors organize their writing. A hiker refers back to the map when he or she is hiking to stay focused on where he or she is going. Writers also need to refer back to the main idea as they write. Just as a guide may take a group to the highest peak, the author wants to help the reader climb to the highest point, or climax, of the story.

Students begin to find their way through the trait of organization by working their way through a maze and reviewing the characteristics of the trait. They practice finding their way through someone else's writing using a sequencing activity. Students then check their own writing for qualities of organization by completing a graphic organizer. The final activity is to plot and sequence a story, then create it.

Finding Your Way in the Maze

Objective

Given the characteristics of the Organization Trait, the student will become familiar with the qualities of organization by completing a maze worksheet.

Standards

- Standard 1A: Uses prewriting strategies to plan written work (e.g., uses graphic organizers), specifically develops awareness of the features of organizational structure

Materials

- Character pattern for classroom display (page 7)
- Finding Your Way in the Maze (page 45)
- Tagboard (optional)
- Backpack, map, compass, boots, etc.

Preparation

Reproduce and enlarge page 7; decorate the pattern as a hiking guide. Reproduce one copy of page 45 onto an overhead transparency and reproduce one paper copy for each student. If desired, make tagboard signposts with trait characteristics to display in the classroom (see the list below).

Lesson Opening

Lead a discussion about story organization by asking the following questions: "Have you ever been lost in the woods? How did you find your way out? Have you reached the end of the story and it seemed like the author never really finished the story? How did that make you feel?"

Lesson Directions

1. Introduce the concept of the Organization Trait using the concept of a hiking guide.
2. Display page 45 on overhead and ask students what they might need to get through the maze of writing. Have the class brainstorm what organization might look like in their writing.
3. Continue to teach the trait of organization, using the optional visual signposts, overhead, or board. Add the characteristics to the hiking guide character pattern for classroom display. Tell students that writing with the trait of organization has . . .
    - a path to lead the reader to the climax
    - clear direction and purpose
    - an attention-getting introduction that grabs the reader
    - a satisfying conclusion that makes the reader think
    - logical order and sequencing of details
    - appropriate pacing
    - transitions that tie together
    - links back to the main idea
4. Distribute page 45 and have students complete the maze. If they finish early, they may design a maze for their partner and write in trait qualities around it.

Lesson Closing

Ask students, "Do you think using these characteristics will help your reader not to get lost when he or she reads your writing?"

Finding Your Way in the Maze *(cont.)*

Directions: Look for the characteristics of organized writing as you complete the maze.

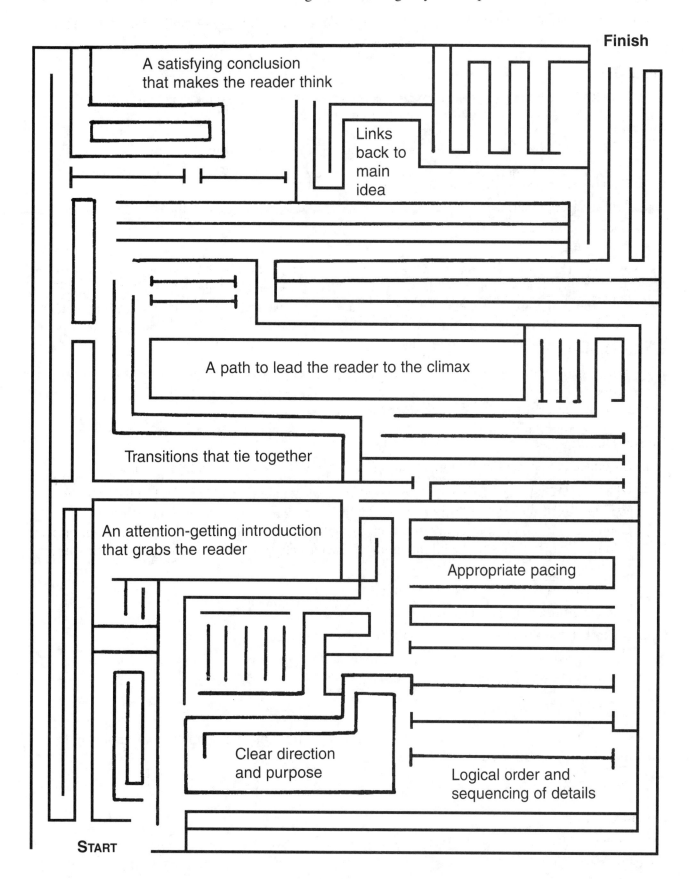

Around the Bend

Objective

Given a read-aloud experience, the student will identify events from the story and put them in proper sequence.

Standards

- Standard 1A: Uses prewriting strategies (e.g., groups related ideas, takes notes)

Materials

- Picture book: *Ira Sleeps Over* by Bernard Waber. Houghton Mifflin, 1972.
- Chapter book option: *The Mouse and the Motorcycle* by Beverly Cleary. William Morrow, 1965.
- Index cards, 6 per student
- Around the Bend (page 47)

Lesson Opening

Ask students, "Have you ever made a whole list of plans for a Saturday?" Then, demonstrate a list on the board as follows: First, I have to clean my room. Then, there is a soccer game at noon, shopping or seeing a friend in the afternoon, etc. "When you make a list like this, do you have a beginning and an end? Do you know why certain things are on the list? Is there a logical order, or do you run from your house to downtown and back out to the mall?"

Lesson Directions

1. Read *Ira Sleeps Over* aloud to the class.

2. Lead a classroom discussion about the story's organization based on the previously taught characteristics.

3. Distribute six index cards to each student. Have them write one event or scene from the story on each card. When they have completed the task, students are to swap their set of cards with a partner. Each student will then put his or her partner's cards in the proper sequence.

4. If you are using the chapter book option, discuss *The Mouse and the Motorcycle* or another book of your choice. After reviewing the plot, have students write key events on the index cards, then proceed as in step 3 above.

5. Distribute page 47 and use it as a review of the Organization Trait.

Lesson Closing

Ask students, "Are you beginning to get a feel for how an author organizes a story? What do you notice about the beginning and the ending of the story?"

Extension Activity

Do the activity again, using the sequencing cards provided from the nonfiction work sample on the next page. (This will probably be more difficult.)

Around the Bend *(cont.)*

Teacher Directions: Fold the page under before making copies so that the answer key does not show.

Student Directions: On separate paper, copy the lines below in an order that makes sense.

1. We went on a hike and saw some elk. We also saw a spider hatching out of an egg.

2. After we left the Silver Lake Visitor Center, we went to Cold Water Lake and had lunch. We also walked around part of the lake.

3. The last thing we did was to eat dinner. My day was very good.

4. Friday we went to Mount St. Helens on a field trip. We went to three different visitor centers.

5. After lunch, we went to the Johnston Ridge Visitor Center. Two things we did were watch a movie and look at a display of a mountain.

6. First, we went to Silver Lake Visitor Center. At the center, we went to a lot of exhibits.

7. Then we went to Cold Water Visitor Center. At the center, we did a scavenger hunt.

8. A few were the time line, the ash fallout, the Ejecta display, the seismograph, and the magma chamber.

Answer Key

1. Friday we went to Mount St. Helens . . .
2. First, we went to Silver Lake Visitor Center . . .
3. A few were the time line, . . .
4. After we left the Silver Lake Visitor Center . . .
5. After lunch . . .

6. We went on a hike . . .
7. Then we went to Cold Water Visitor Center . . .
8. The last thing we did . . .

Getting Organized

Objective

Given a graphic organizer, the student will complete it using a sample of his or her actual writing.

Standards

- Standard 1A: Uses prewriting strategies to plan written work (e.g., uses graphic organizers, groups related ideas, takes notes, brainstorms ideas)
- Standard 1B: Uses strategies to draft and revise written work (e.g., elaborates on a central idea, uses paragraphs to develop separate ideas)
- Standard 1D: Evaluates own writing (e.g., identifies the best features of a piece of writing, determines how own writing achieves its purposes)

Materials

- Student-generated rough drafts from previous assignments
- Getting Organized, page 49
- Hiker character pattern on classroom display

Preparation

Reproduce one copy of page 49 on an overhead transparency. Reproduce one or two copies of page 49 for each student.

Lesson Opening

Ask students, "If a reader was hiking through the maze of your words, would he or she get lost? Why or why not?"

Lesson Directions

1. Discuss and review characteristics of organization, using page 49 as an overhead, the hiker character pattern on classroom display, and any other visual aids (e.g., signposts).
2. Distribute copies of page 49 and rough drafts of student work, if students do not have them readily accessible in their notebooks.
3. Have students complete the graphic organizer, using elements from their rough drafts.
4. Ask students to add or make changes to their graphic organizer as needed. Explain that these changes will help them in rewriting later.
5. If time allows, students may rewrite their story incorporating changes from the graphic organizer.

Lesson Closing

Ask students how this exercise helped them organize their thoughts and their story. What kinds of changes did they need to make?

Getting Organized *(cont.)*

Directions: Use this graphic organizer to improve a piece of writing or to get started on a new draft.

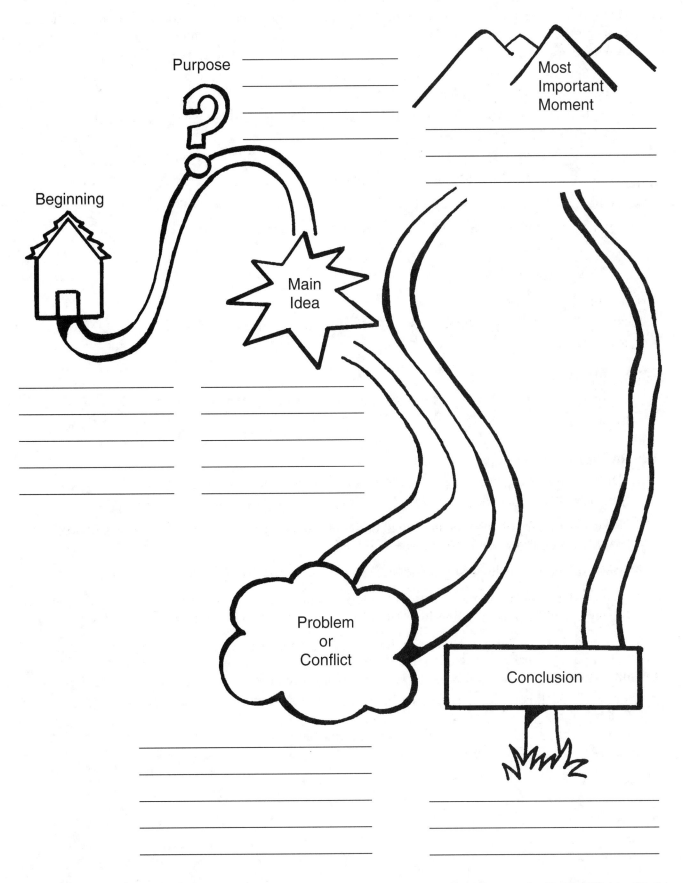

Purpose

Beginning

Most Important Moment

Main Idea

Problem or Conflict

Conclusion

Beginnings and Endings

Objective

Given sample leads and conclusions from literature, the student will identify what makes them effective by discussing them with a partner. Then, given sample beginnings and endings from student work, the student will rewrite them with a partner to make the leads and conclusions more effective.

Standards

- Standard 1D: Evaluates others' writing (e.g., identifies the best features of a piece of writing, responds to classmates' writing)
- Standard 2C: Identifies and becomes aware of a variety of sentence structures

Materials

- Beginnings and Endings (pages 51–52)

Preparation

Reproduce pages 51–52 on overhead transparencies.

Lesson Opening

Read aloud the following story beginning: *Once upon a time there was a boy named Bob.* Ask students if they want to hear any more of the story. Why or why not?

Lesson Directions

1. Ask students what kind of story beginning makes them want to keep reading. How might an author get the reader's attention? Brainstorm these qualities as a class and list on the board or the overhead. Include concepts from the Organization Trait in the discussion.

2. Read aloud and/or display on overhead leads from literature (page 51) and discuss.

3. Ask students what makes a "satisfying conclusion." What do we mean when we say that? Does the author abruptly say "the end" because he or she is tired of writing and/or it is time for recess? Read aloud some sample conclusions from literature (page 52). Ask students if they would want to read more. Did the author make them think? How?

4. Ask students to write one sample lead and one sample conclusion. Ask students to omit their names from their papers. Collect the leads and conclusions.

5. Distribute anonymous sample student leads and conclusions. Have partner groups edit and/or rewrite them, incorporating qualities from the Organization Trait.

6. Select pairs to share rewritten beginnings and endings with the class. Ask students if the writing is more effective now. Refer back to the discussion questions used in the beginning of the lesson.

Lesson Closing

Ask students what they have learned about writing leads and conclusions for their stories. Ask them what makes this part of writing easy or difficult.

Beginnings and Endings *(cont.)*

Directions: Discuss the following story beginnings from literature.

1. "Julie was skipping home from school. She came to a large moving van." (*David's Father*, Robert Munsch. Annick Press, 1983.)

2. "One Friday Miss Nelson told her class that she was going to have her tonsils out." (*Miss Nelson is Missing*, Harry Allard and James Marshall. Houghton Mifflin, 1977.)

3. "I'm worried about Harry." (*Song Lee and the Leech Man*, Suzy Kline. Viking, 1995.)

4. "On Christmas Eve, many years ago, I lay quietly in my bed." (*The Polar Express*, Chris Van Allsburg. Houghton Mifflin, 1985.)

5. "It was not that Omri didn't appreciate Patrick's birthday present to him. Far from it." (*The Indian in the Cupboard*, Lynne Reid Banks. Avon Books, 1980.)

6. "Each day Mark Anderson told himself he would not stop that night." (*Gentle Ben*, Walt Morey. Avon Books, 1965.)

7. "Jeremy Thatcher crumpled his paper in disgust." (*Jeremy Thatcher, Dragon Hatcher*, Bruce Coville. Pocket Books, Simon & Schuster, 1991.)

8. "Brian opened the door and stood back." (*The River*, Gary Paulsen. Bantam Doubleday Dell Books, 1991.)

9. "Not long ago in a large university town in California, on a street called Orchard Avenue, a strange old man ran a dusty shabby store." (*The Egypt Game*, Zilpha K. Snyder. Bantam Doubleday Dell Books, 1967.)

10. "It was almost December, and Jonas was beginning to be frightened." (*The Giver*, Lois Lowry. Bantam Doubleday Dell Books for Young Readers, 1993.)

Beginnings and Endings *(cont.)*

Directions: Read and discuss the following endings from literature.

1. "They decided not to mention Miss Viola Swamp. But they wondered why Miss Nelson hadn't seen her in the hall." (*Miss Nelson is Missing*, Harry Allard and James Marshall. Houghton Mifflin, 1977.)

2. "'You think he is scary?' said David. 'Wait till you meet my grandmother.'" (*David's Father*, Robert Munsch. Annick Press, 1983.)

3. "I bet I know what she wished for on her tiny piece of yellow paper." (*Song Lee and the Leech Man*, Suzy Kline. Viking, 1995.)

4. "At the last moment, as you flash overhead, he will suddenly rear to his full heart-stopping height and present a never-to-be-forgotten picture of great jaws sprung wide and huge forepaws thrust up, as if with one mighty sweep he would brush your plane from the sky." (*Gentle Ben*, Walt Morey. Avon Books, 1965.)

5. "'Then he took out some paper and began to draw." (*Jeremy Thatcher, Dragon Hatcher*, Bruce Coville. Pocket Books, Simon & Schuster, 1991.)

6. "'Next time,' he read aloud, 'it won't be so hard to paddle. Thanks.'" (*The River*, Gary Paulsen. Bantam Doubleday Dell Books, 1991.)

7. "'Melanie,' she said, 'what do you know about gypsies?'" (*The Egypt Game*, Zilpha K. Snyder. Bantam Doubleday Dell Books, 1967.)

8. "Behind him, across vast distances of space and time, from the place he had left, he thought he heard music echo. But perhaps it was only an echo." (*The Giver*, Lois Lowry. Bantam Doubleday Dell Books for Young Readers, 1993.)

9. "'Anything to eat?' cried Charlie, laughing, 'Oh, you just wait and see!'" (*Charlie and the Chocolate Factory*, Roald Dahl. Puffin Books, 1964.)

10. "'Shhh, yes. There's a rumor going around that the beautiful girl arriving today might be the queen they've been waiting for.'" (*Bridge to Terabithia*, Katherine Paterson. Avon Books, 1977.)

Will Your Story Be a Classic?

Objective

Given a simple story model, the student will plot out and write a story within a small group setting.

Standards

- Standard 1A: Uses prewriting strategies to plan written work (e.g., uses graphic organizers and story maps; groups related ideas; takes notes; brainstorms ideas)
- Standard 1B: Uses strategies to draft and revise written work (e.g., elaborates on a central idea; writes with attention to voice, audience, word choice, tone, and imagery; uses paragraphs to develop separate ideas)
- Standard 1H: Writes narrative accounts (e.g., engages the reader by establishing a context and otherwise developing reader interest; establishes a situation, plot, point of view, setting, and conflict; creates an organizational structure that balances and unifies all narrative aspects of the story; uses sensory details and concrete language to develop plot and character; uses a range of strategies such as dialogue and tension or suspense)

Materials

- Sticky notes
- Tagboard, enough sheets to distribute to small groups

Lesson Opening

Ask students, "Are you ready to put on your hiking boots and guide someone through your writing from beginning to end?"

Lesson Directions

1. Review the characteristics of the Organization Trait. Ask students to think about their favorite Disney movies and/or classic stories such as *The Wizard of Oz*. Ask students to identify patterns, types of characters that recur, the steps in the process as the hero tries to solve his or her problem or meet a challenge set before him or her. Have them think about how the stories end. Are they always happy endings? List each story element on the overhead or board as it is discussed. Use the story outline on page 54, if needed, to prompt discussion.

2. Ask students how the current discussion ties in with the trait of organization. What are the similarities between the movie/story outline as discussed in class and the characteristics of the trait?

3. Divide the class into groups of 4–5 students. Give each group sticky notes and a sheet of tag board.

4. Have the students plot out a story. Encourage them to make up their own characters, events, etc. Display the posters you created from "Write Your Own Script" (page 33) if needed, as prompts. Students should write one action or event per sticky note and then place them in story order on the tagboard.

5. Students can then write out the story, using their group's sticky notes as a guide.

Lesson Closing

Ask students how organizing the pieces of the story first helped them in their writing. You might want to have students retain their stories to use as rough drafts and to complete the writing process through editing and publishing another time.

Story Outline Questions for Guided Class Discussion

- What types of characters are in the story? Are there good characters? bad characters? Is the hero or heroine perfect or flawed?

- What are the patterns in the story?

- What does your main character want? What problems does he or she encounter? What steps will he or she take to solve the problem(s)? Does anyone help or hinder the main character along the way? Is there any danger?

- What role does the "bad guy" play?

- How does the character overcome the difficulty?

- How does the story end? Does it always end "happily ever after"?

- Does the hero or heroine reach the desired goal? Why or why not? Is there more than one part to the conclusion?

Conventions Trait

A word formerly used for *conventions* is *mechanics*; teachers at one time referred to the "mechanics of writing." This section explores the job of a mechanic and how it relates to writing. Conventions are the writer's tools to keep his or her crafted story running smoothly. Because editing is a big job, students will learn to be mechanics and fix their writing, using one tool at a time. They will find that it takes practice to become familiar with using the tools. Students will be encouraged to revise, or improve, their writing, as well as correct mistakes.

Conventions, as identified in this six-trait model, include spelling, punctuation, capitalization, grammar, paragraphs, and using appropriate titles. The teacher may also address repetition or overuse of words, the correct use of *that* and *which*, using active verbs instead of "to be" verbs, and using descriptive nouns to cut down on overuse of adjectives.

In the first lesson, students will learn what the conventions are and will be introduced to common proofreading marks to use in editing. They will have the opportunity to practice in a whole-class exercise using the overhead before trying their hand at editing a writing sample. Students will go on to edit a longer piece of writing in the next lesson, focusing on just one convention at a time. They will have one more opportunity to practice editing someone else's work in class before beginning to edit their own work. While students initially will focus on one convention at a time when editing their own work, in the fourth lesson students are asked to look more closely at their entire work, using a series of questions. The final lesson in this section gives students the opportunity to rewrite their work as final copy and to consider publishing options for their writing.

Using a Writer's Tools

Objective

Given the meaning of proofreading marks and a copy of a writing sample, the student will edit the piece using appropriate proofreading marks.

Standards

- Standard 1C: Uses strategies to edit written work (e.g., edits for grammar, punctuation, capitalization, and spelling at a developmentally appropriate level; considers page format [paragraphs, titles])
- Standard 1D: Evaluates others' writing
- Standard 3: Uses grammatical and mechanical conventions in written compositions

Materials

- Character pattern for classroom display (page 7)
- Writer's Tool Box (page 58)
- Paragraph Repair Shop (page 59)
- Common Proofreading Marks (page 60)
- Writing Sample (page 61)
- Tape or sticky fabric dots
- Red pens
- Tools, coveralls, old rags, etc.

Preparation

Reproduce and enlarge page 7 and decorate it as a mechanic. Reproduce one copy of page 58 and cut it apart to display around the mechanic for classroom display, enlarging it as necessary. Reproduce page 60 onto an overhead with the far right hand column covered.

Lesson Opening

Tell students that although they will be hearing about the Conventions Trait, conventions at one time were known as mechanics and teachers used to refer to the "mechanics of writing." Ask students, "What are mechanics? What do they do? What do they use to the fix the problem? Are there any tools a writer can use to fix his or her writing?"

Lesson Directions

1. Introduce the Conventions Trait with examples from a broken car. Ask students, if you had a flat tire, what tools might you use to fix it? What if the battery cable were loose and the car wouldn't start? What other tools might you use to work on a car? What if you have a piece of "broken" writing? How would you fix it?

Using a Writer's Tools *(cont.)*

Lesson Directions *(cont.)*

2. Teach the trait. Tell students that to edit means to correct, or fix, a piece of writing, including the following:

   - Spelling
   - Capitalization
   - Punctuation
   - Paragraphs
   - Grammar

   - Title
   - Repetition, over-use of words
   - Correct word usage, e.g., "that" and "which"
   - Using active verbs, instead of "to be"
   - Employing descriptive nouns rather than adjectives

3. Show the first overhead sample of writing that needs to be edited, or "repaired" (page 59). Ask students what needs to be fixed and what tools should be used (e.g., capitals—wrench, periods—nuts and bolts, spelling—screwdriver). As students state each convention, show the class the appropriate tool tag and have student volunteers use tape or sticky fabric dots to attach the tag around the mechanic character pattern on classroom display.

4. Ask students if they want to add other tools from the lesson to the mechanic on display that haven't already been posted.

5. Teach the proofreader's marks (page 60). Display the overhead of Common Proofreading Marks. Write in the appropriate symbol as you talk about each one. Explain that these will be the students' "tools."

6. Display additional sample paragraph(s) on the overhead one at a time for further practice, if needed.

Lesson Closing

Ask students, "What do we mean when we talk about conventions?" (Tools we use to correct our writing, or the "mechanics" of writing.) "Which are the hardest for you to remember to use in your own writing? Which are the easiest?"

Extension

Distribute the writing sample (page 61) to students. Ask which writer's tools are needed to edit the piece. Have students use red pens to correct it. The sample provided has 21 corrections to be made. Tell students that two of the corrections will be writing a title and a satisfying conclusion.

Writer's Tool Box

Directions: Reproduce and cut the sheet apart to use as part of the classroom display described on page 57.

Capitals

Punctuation

Spelling

Paragraphs

Grammar

Paragraph Repair Shop

Directions: Read the following paragraphs and make the corrections.

There is many kinds of cars and trucks. Sometimes a car quits runing and needs to be repaired A mechanic fix cars. He sues different Tools to work on them. A mechanics most useful tool is pliers wrench screwdriver. It is important for his to use the right tool to do the job.

The tire on my car was flat yesterday. I puled over to the side of the road. Then I opened the trunk and got the jack out. The nuts on the tires were too tight for me to get lose, so I used a spechal tol that is called a star wrench. Changing a tire is hard work.

Writers use tools, too. They need to fix their writing to make it better. easier for people to read. Speling and puctuation are to important writing tools. It is also important to put Capitals why they belong.

Paragraph Repair Shop

Common Proofreading Marks

Capitals		Capitalize Make lower case
Punctuation		Period Comma Exclamation Point Question Mark Quotation Marks
Spelling		Insert letter or word left out
Paragraphs		Start new paragraph Combine paragraphs
Grammar		Switch word or phrase order (to make better sense) Delete

Writing Sample

[Title?]

Once upon a time there was two brothers. They lived in a cream colored house surrounded by towering fir trees every morning they fought because one of them liked to get up early and the other wanted to Sleep in.

One day, Thomas decided to solve the problem. He tied a thin string to the light switch.

"Now I need the black rope," he mutered to himself. "Where is it, Keith?"

"Don't ask me. Look in the junk bucket. Or maybe under your bed."

Thomas rumaged around and soon pulled out a thick rope. He tied it to the thin string, and looped it across the hammock hanging over the bed he walked back and forth across the room, from the bed to the light switch, testing his invintion.

"Look, Mom!" he called I can lay in bed and turn the light off."

"That's not fair," Keith said. "I'm going to rig up a way to turn the light on again. Thomas have you seen my rope?"

"It's probably in the bucket, where I found mine. You look."

Head down, rump in the air, Keith began tossing things out of the bucket.

"Woo hoo!" He held up a red rope. "Look thomas. Now I'm going to tie it on to your string and when you turn the light off I can turn it back on!"

"Keith tied the rope to the string on the light switch he stretched the rope across the floor to his bed. Thomas started testing the invention by pulling on his rope to turn the light on and off. But . . . the smal string kept falling off the ligth switch. He tied some knots and arranged strings and ropes around the hammock and back to his bed. At last he got it to work.

"Hey, Mom! Come here!"

[Write a satisfying conclusion.]

One Tool at a Time

Objective

Given writing samples and cue cards, the student will practice editing for conventions, focusing on one element at a time.

Standards

- Standard 1C: Uses strategies to edit written work (e.g., edits for grammar, punctuation, capitalization, and spelling at a developmentally appropriate level; considers page format [paragraphs, indentations, titles])
- Standard 1D: Evaluates others' writing
- Standard 3: Uses grammatical and mechanical conventions in written compositions

Materials

- Colored construction paper
- Colored pencils
- Six tools as shown on page 58 (optional)
- Writing Samples (pages 63–68)
- Mechanic character pattern on classroom display

Preparation

Cut the colored paper into large cue cards and label each one as follows: spelling, capitalization, grammar, paragraphs, and title. You may wish to create a packet using pages 63–68 for each student for ease in completing the "assembly line" exercise (see #3, below).

Lesson Opening

Draw the students' attention to the mechanic and tool display created in the previous lesson. Ask if a mechanic learns to use all the tools at once, or one at a time. Explain to the students that they will learn to recognize the conventions one at a time in editing.

Lesson Directions

1. Review the conventions poster and proofreading marks.
2. Divide the class into six groups.
3. Explain the following "assembly line" activity: each group starts with a cue card (and appropriate tool, if available) and the corresponding writing sample. Allow 5–10 minutes to edit the appropriate sample, correcting only the convention represented by that card and tool. At the end of work period, each group passes the cue card (and tool) to the next group, and everyone turns to the appropriate page. You may wish to have students use colored pencils, preferably in the same color as card, to edit. Direct students to do some of the work individually and some as a group.

Lesson Closing

Ask the class how it felt to practice using the tools one at a time. Ask students to review the tools by holding the tools one at a time and asking students to name a convention to look for when editing.

Writing Sample for Using the Spelling Tool

Directions: Find the spelling errors. Write the word correctly above the incorrectly spelled word.

Jonathon lay back on his bed and stared at the knoted pine boards above. David, his twin, lounghed on the floor. The attic loft room, with the fan blowing across him, was the place to be on a warm summer day, Jonathan reflected, especialy if none of the guys were around to play baseball or ride bikes. Pale blue walls reflected light from the window back into the room. The mulberry tree nearby ofered shade from the heat of the day.

Lazely, Jonathon let his eyes roam over each of the boards, one by one. Suddenly he stopped.

"David, look! That board. It's diferint."

"Oh, it's just a knothole." David fiddled with the string in his hands.

Puzzled, Jonathon stared at the board. "It's shaped like a key. It even looks as if there's a metel plate around it, like a keyhole for a door."

"No," David said, "The wood's just darker there, or looks darker because of the hole. It's nothing out of the ordinery."

Jonathon kept looking at the hole. It certainly looked like a keyhole. "I wonder," he mused, "if I had a key and turned it in the keyhole, would a door or a panle open?" The only way to find out was to get a key and try it.

Jonathon sat up and swung his legs over the edge of the bed. He walked over to the desk and pulled the chair across the floor so that it was positined directly under the hole.

Writing Sample for Using the Capitalization Tool

Directions: Correct errors in capitalization using proofreader's marks.

"Move, David." Standing on the chair, Jonathon reached up to feel the hole. he took his bike lock key out of his pocket and tried it in the keyhole.

"That doesn't come close to fitting," David protested.

Jonathon got off the chair and pushed it back over to the desk. "No," he said, "before I look for a key, I need to know what I'm looking for." He pushed the chair back over to the hole. Then he walked over to the desk, rummaged around, and found a piece of paper and a pencil.

"What are you doing?"

"You'll see." Jonathon climbed back up on the chair, holding the paper and pencil. he had to stand on tiptoe to reach the keyhole; even then, he had to reach up and lean his head back—it was most awkward, but he managed to get a key shape traced.

"Now I'm ready to find the key!" in his enthusiasm, Jonathon forgot about the midday heat.

He ran down the stairs and banged out the screen door. david followed at a more leisurely pace and caught up with Jonathon on the porch.

"Where am I going to look first?" Staring out towards the mulberry tree, jonathon straddled the porch railing and pondered the best place to begin looking for a key. "I know! i'll go down and check around the basement."

"at least it's cool down there," David said.

Writing Sample for Using the Punctuation Tool

Directions: Find punctuation errors. Show the correct punctuation using proofreader's marks.

The two boys went around to the side of the house The cool musty odor of the basement greeted Jonathan as he opened the door. He went down the narrow step slowly allowing his eyes time to adjust to the darkness. Jonathon rounded the post at the bottom of the stairs and glanced at the shelves. He couldn't decide whether or not to search them thoroughly. Deciding not to, he turned around to survey the rest of the basement and almost bumped into David.

"It's too dark to look very well down here," Jonathon said. I'll never find a key in this mess. If I did, it probably would be rusted and corroded and wouldn't work. He sighed and went up the stairs as slowly as he had gone down.

"Maybe the shop would be a good place to look" David suggested as they stepped around the corner into the backyard. The door to the shop was open, as usual, and Jonathon walked in. Now this, this was a fascinating place, even if it was messy.

"I've got to get serious about finding this key before dinner." Jonathon said "After dinner, I want to play ball with the guys." Jonathon looked around as David stopped to fool with some tools on the workbench. Jonathon didn't see any keys on the workbench. He walked over to look at the pegboard, and sure enough, a key was hanging there Jonathon looked at the key for a minute, studying it.

"It doesn't look like it fits the garage door, but I'll try it to be sure before I take it."

Writing Sample for Using the Grammar Tool

Directions: Find errors in grammar. Correct them by using proofreader's marks and writing the correct words or phrases over the incorrect ones.

Discovering that the key don't work in the garage door, he slipped it into the pocket of his jeans.

"Time to go see if this key works!" He jogged across the lawn and up the back porch. The screen door bang shut behind him.

"Wait for me!" David all of a sudden bursted through the door and it slammed a second time.

Bounding the stairs two at a time, Jonathon turned on the landing and continued up the second flight of stairs. He hesitate when he got to his room, uncertain what would happen when he tried the key in the keyhole. The room looked the same as always, the chair just as he had left it, the shadows from the tree branches a little longer in the afternoon sun. Jonathon taked the key out of his pocket and climbed up on the chair.

"Here goes." He tried the key in the hole. It went in halfway, then stopped.

"Let me try," David said. He took the key, turned it over, and tried again. It wouldn't begin to go in the keyhole this time.

Jonathon took a folded piece of paper out of his pocket.

"Guess I should have checked the key shape against this tracing before I came back in the house. Now I have to start all over again looking for a key." He sit down on the edge of the bed, rest his chin in his hands, and stared out the window.

"I'm going outside," David said. "Come on, let's play catch."

Writing Sample for Using the Paragraphs Tool

Directions: Find paragraph breaks and show them using proofreader's marks.

"Okay. When we get together with the guys after dinner, I can ask them where else to look for an old key that would fit." David had just tossed the ball to Jonathon when Michael sauntered by. "Hey, what'cha doing? Are we playing ball tonight?" "Yeah, I guess so," Michael answered. "We're short a few, though. The Grays are out of town, and John has to go somewhere with his folks." "Well," Jonathon said slowly, still not sure if he wanted to let anyone else help him discover what might lie behind the keyhole. "I know of something else we could do." "What?" Jonathon showed Michael the tracing of the key and tried to explain. "Hmm, I don't know. I guess we can look for a key." "Dinner!" "We've got to go," Jonathon said. "Let's meet back here at 6:30 and we'll decide then what to do." Thump, thump. Jonathon smacked the ball into his glove as he waited. "Hi there. What's this I hear about a key?" "Hi, Paul," Jonathon said. "I'll explain when everyone gets here." Just then Michael walked up. "It looks like the only one we're waiting for now is Dan," he said.

"Speaking of . . . ," Jonathon grinned, as Dan turned a sharp corner into Jonathon's yard on his bike.

"Okay," Michael said. "Tell us about the key."

Writing Sample for Using the Title Tool

Directions: This page does not need any specific corrections. You will need to read pages 63–68 before you can write a satisfying conclusion. Once you have done so, read the story from beginning to end and write a title that will grab your reader's attention.

Jonathon took the paper out of his pocket again. "I know it sounds crazy, guys," he said. "Today I noticed a keyhole in one of the boards in the ceiling of my room. David thinks it's a knothole, but it's not. I made a tracing, see?" He held out the paper. "It has a metal plate around it, like a door has. I thought if we find a key that fits, we could open it and see what's behind the door or panel."

"I'm game!" Paul exclaimed. "Let's go!"

"Wait, wait. Let's go check out this keyhole first. Maybe we don't want to see what's behind the panel."

"Michael, you're too cautious! Who cares? Let me see that tracing. Let's plan where to look." Recklessly, Dan threw his bike down and grabbed the paper.

Intercepting quickly so Jonathon could salvage the tracing, David said, "I think Michael has a good idea. Let's all go up and look at the keyhole. That will give us a better idea what to do next."

"Okay," they all agreed. "Lead on, Jonathon." Five boys banged through the screen door and thumped up the stairs. Bursting into Jonathon's room, Paul plopped faceup on the bed.

"Sure, guys, here it is. Metal plate and all, just like he said."

_____

_____

_____

_____

_____

_____

_____

_____

Working with Tools

Objective

Given a review of conventions, the student will edit his or her work one step at a time, becoming more familiar with editing in the process.

Standards

- Standard 1C: Uses strategies to edit written work (e.g., edits for grammar, punctuation, capitalization, and spelling at a developmentally appropriate level; considers page format [paragraphs, margins, indentations, titles], selects presentation format)
- Standard 1D: Evaluates others' writing (e.g., identifies the best features of a piece of writing, determines how own writing achieves its purposes, asks for feedback)
- Standard 3: Uses grammatical and mechanical conventions in written compositions

Materials

- Mechanic character pattern for classroom display
- Writing Sample—Putting It Altogether (page 70)
- Student-generated rough drafts from any previous lesson
- Colored pencils or red pencils
- Colored overhead markers or a red overhead marker
- Dictionaries, student spelling books, or other spelling aids
- Overhead marking pens in colors corresponding to tool cue cards (page 58)

Preparation

Reproduce page 70 on a transparency as well as a copy of page 70 for each student.

Lesson Opening

Tell students that once a mechanic is familiar with all of his or her tools, he or she can only work on one thing at a time, even though everything in a motor is connected. As writers edit, correcting one convention at a time, their writing may not look like much. Like a repaired motor, however, when the editing is complete, the story comes back together.

Lesson Directions

1. Discuss with students how sometimes it's difficult to remember all the conventions when editing, or correcting, our work.
2. Review the mechanic poster on display, and also go over proofreading marks with students.
3. Edit one convention at a time on the overhead transparency, using colors that correspond to the colors of the cue cards that you created for the lesson on page 58. Ask students to use the same color of pencil to edit their own work in the same manner. (If this is not possible, use a red marker and pencils for corrections.)
4. Begin with spelling. Continue with punctuation, grammar, capitalization, and marking paragraphs. Conclude with creating titles.
5. Have students decide on a plan to carry out to publish their work.

Lesson Closing

Show the overhead of the edited sample with all of the colored corrections; discuss how the piece has come together through the editing process. Ask students, "Is it easier to tackle the big job of editing when correcting only one thing at a time?"

Writing Sample—Putting It Altogether

This is my perfect planet. my planet

would be called indefectibility. It would

hve 100 peopl and all of my friends.

would be there I would also have lots of

varity of animals. There would be lots

of skybat. and other dinosaurs. There

would be mountain lions, lions, toads,

frogs, insects, mammles, etc. The

animals would have the same language as us. The planet would have lots of plants. But it would not

have any of the poisenous plants like, poisen oak, poisen ivy, stinging nettle, etc. All the plants would

be eatable. There would be forests. The planet would also have no pollution and lots of rings and

moons. There would be 7 moons and all of them would be different colors. There would be all the

colors of the rainbow on the rings. There would be good teachers who teach spelling, social studies,

how to use the play equipment, etc. that would be my perfect planet, because that's what I like that

doesn't always happen here. The planet would be bigger than Jupitor. and warm snow That would be

my perfect planet.

—*Kenneth Mabry (used with author's permission)*

Becoming a Professional Mechanic

Objective

Given a series of steps ("Levels"), the student will complete a process of revision by making changes to his or her writing.

Standards

- Standard 1B: Uses strategies to draft and revise written work (e.g., elaborates on a central idea; writes with attention to voice, audience, word choice, tone, and imagery; uses paragraphs to develop separate ideas)
- Standard 1D: Evaluates own and others' writing (e.g., identifies the best features of a piece of writing, determines how own writing achieves its purposes, asks for feedback)
- Standard 2A: Uses descriptive language that clarifies and enhances ideas
- Standard 2C: Uses a variety of sentence structures
- Standard 3: Uses grammatical and mechanical conventions in written compositions

Materials

- Five sheets of tagboard and large marker
- Levels of Revision (page 72)
- Rough drafts of student writing, typed if possible
- Model car and/or cutaway diagrams of a car (optional)

Preparation

Refer to page 72 to create one poster for each level. Decorate the poster with cutaway diagrams of a car, if desired.

Lesson Opening

Tell students it is time now for a major engine overhaul. In many repair jobs, the mechanic must take out some exterior parts to fix the internal problem. We can approach revising the same way, from the exterior of the piece of writing to its core.

Lesson Directions

1. Explain/review the difference between "editing" and "revising": editing corrects a piece, while revising changes it for the better.

2. Go over the five levels of revision displayed on the posters. Then display only the card for Level 1. Point out that everyone has already done the first step, letting the writing sit, taking a vacation from the piece, as it were. As students work through the process, you may want to have them work with a partner. Let them work for 10–15 minutes, monitoring as necessary.

3. Give an appropriate signal to let the class know it's time to move on to Level 2. Display the corresponding poster card and check for understanding before students begin revising. Continue to answer student questions as they work. Give the class another 10–15 minutes before signaling to move on to Level 3. Continue the process through each level, checking for understanding, monitoring student progress, and answering questions as necessary.

Lesson Closing

Ask students if they feel like their writing is in pieces. Which level was the hardest or easiest for them to complete? Why? Did they find that thinking through the specific guidelines helped them improve their writing?

Levels of Revision

Level 1

- Let the piece sit—overnight or longer, if possible.
- Read the piece all the way through.
- Read it. Change it. Read it. Change it.
- Does it sound complete? Is there a part missing?

Level 2

- Look a little closer.
- Check the focus.
- Cut out whatever does not relate to the main topic.
- Does the ending answer any questions raised in the beginning?
- Does the piece say what you intended to say?

Level 3

- Take the piece apart a little more.
- Is it logically organized?
- Cut out any self-conscious writing.
- Remember that your reader will filter your writing through his or her personal experience.
- Read it aloud. Cut out anything that doesn't sound right.

Level 4

- Look at the details.
- Read it aloud—slowly. Look for awkward sentence structure.
- Check for any long sentences that should be two sentences instead.
- Does every line add to the whole?

Level 5

- Time to get down to the nuts and bolts.
- Cut out any extra words that don't add to the whole.
- Change/add words for clarification.
- Look for repeated words. Use a thesaurus to add interest.
- Look up words to check meanings and spelling.
- Line edit—make sure every sentence, phrase, and word says what you want.

Putting It Back Together

Objective
Given a piece of edited writing, the student will publish a final copy.

Standards
- Standard 1C: Uses strategies to edit written work (e.g., edits for grammar, punctuation, capitalization, and spelling at a developmentally appropriate level; considers page format [paragraphs, margins, indentations, titles], selects presentation format, incorporates illustrations)
- Standard 1F: Writes stories or essays that convey an intended purpose (e.g., to record ideas, to describe, to explain)
- Standard 2: Demonstrates competence in the stylistic and rhetorical aspects of writing
- Standard 3: Uses grammatical and mechanical conventions in written compositions

Materials
- Student writing samples used in "Becoming a Professional Mechanic"
- Nuts and bolts, or similar small mechanical parts (for demonstration)
- Samples of "published" student work, if available

Lesson Opening
Demonstrate to the class putting nuts and bolts together by using tools or a similar illustration of putting something together. Explain that now they are ready to put all the pieces of their edited writing together, rewritten as a final, complete copy.

Lesson Directions
1. Review the steps of the writing process: pre-writing, writing, revising, editing, and publishing. Discuss how the class has completed all but the final step, publishing.

2. Allow the class time to work on writing a final copy, using the changes made in the editing and revising lessons. Monitor student work for neatness, accuracy, and completeness.

3. Have students brainstorm ways their work could be published. Ideas may vary depending on the nature of writing completed. Suggestions include creating a class book, a magazine for the school library or a community business to put in their waiting area, illustrated stories to give to younger children, bookmarks, or cards (if students have poetry to publish).

Lesson Closing
Ask students how it feels to have completed a piece of writing, from start to finish. Are they more satisfied, more pleased with the final copy than they were the rough draft? Why? Is the process worth it?

Six-Trait Revue

Objective

Given visual cues and auditory input, the student will review the six traits by creating cards and a rap song or poem to depict the characteristics of his or her trait to present to the class.

Standards

- Standard 1: Demonstrates awareness of the general skills and strategies of the writing process
- Standard 2: Demonstrates awareness of the stylistic and rhetorical aspects of writing
- Standard 4F: Uses graphic organizers to gather and record information
- Standard 4G: Compiles information into oral reports

Materials

- Cards on which to write characteristics of each trait
- Character patterns for classroom display from each of the six traits

Lesson Opening

Tell students, "We've been living with the traits now for a number of weeks. On stage today, we'll have some helpers to bring them back to you again. Remember to show respect for your fellow classmates during the presentations."

Lesson Directions

1. Review the traits, using classroom posters on display.

2. Place students into six groups and assign each one a trait. Distribute cards on which they are to write the characteristics of their trait. Students can use classroom posters, any notes from previous lessons, and other classroom resource materials to help them.

3. Have students write a song or poem with illustrations, actions, movements, etc., for their trait, using words and concepts from the class posters and lessons.

4. Have each group present their trait to the class.

Lesson Closing

Say to students, "Now that we've become a little more familiar with each trait, hopefully it will be easier to remember to include these qualities in our writing. Which trait is easiest for you to incorporate in your own writing? Why? Which trait is the most difficult? What have you learned during these lessons that will help you develop those characteristics in your own writing? Let's give a hand to the traits!" (Applaud the class for their performances.)

Answer Key

Pages 39–40: Voices are from the following individuals. Your students will present a wide variety of answers. Accept reasonable responses.

1. middle-aged female, writer (permission granted by Susan G. Wooldridge, November 1999)
2. 42-year-old male, youth worker, speaker (permission granted by Dennis Blackwell, April 2000)
3. 82-year-old female, retired librarian (permission granted by Helen Lantis, April 2000)
4. 15-year-old female, student (permission granted by Amber Mullins, April 2000)
5. 11-year-old male, student (permission granted by Kenneth Mabry, April 2000)

Note to the teacher: You may wish to copy the corrected paragraphs and pages that follow onto overheads to display to students for correcting their own work, or you may make regular paper copies to give to students for the same purpose.

Page 45

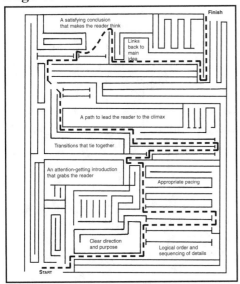

Page 59

There are many kinds of cars and trucks. Sometimes a car quits running and needs to be repaired. A mechanic fixes cars. He uses different tools to work on them. A mechanic's most useful tools are pliers, a wrench, and a screwdriver. It is important for him to use the right tool to do the job.

The tire on my car was flat yesterday. I pulled over to the side of the road. Then I opened the trunk and got the jack out. The nuts on the tires were to tight for me to get loose, so I used a special tool that is called a star wrench. Changing a tire is hard work.

Writers use tools, too. They need to fix their writing to make it better and easier for people to read. Spelling and punctuation are important writing tools. It is also important to put capitals where they belong.

Page 61 (Corrections include title and conclusion. Student titles and ending will vary. Have students check their conclusion against the traits of organization.)

[Title]

Once upon a time there **were** two brothers. They lived in a cream colored house surrounded by towering fir trees. **E**very morning they fought because one of them liked to get up early and the other wanted to **s**leep in.

One day, Thomas decided to solve the problem. He tied a thin string to the light switch.

"Now I need the black rope,**"** he **muttered** to himself. "Where is it, Keith?"

"Don't ask me. Look in the junk bucket. Or maybe under your bed."

Thomas **rummaged** around and soon pulled out a thick rope. He tied it to the thin string, and looped it across the hammock hanging over the bed. **H**e walked back and forth across the room, from the bed to the light switch, testing his **invention**.

"Look, Mom!" he called, "**I** can lay in bed and turn the light off."

"That's not fair," Keith said. "I'm going to rig up a way to turn the light on again. Thomas, have you seen my rope?"

"It's probably in the bucket, where I found mine. You look."

Answer Key *(cont.)*

Head down, rump in the air, Keith began tossing things out of the bucket.

"Woo hoo!" He held up a red rope. "Look Thomas. Now I'm going to tie it on to your string, and when you turn the light off, I can turn it back on!"

"Keith tied the rope to the string on the light switch. **He** stretched the rope across the floor to his bed. Thomas started testing the invention by pulling on his rope to turn the light on and off. But . . . the **small** string kept falling off the **light** switch. He tied some knots and arranged strings and ropes around the hammock and back to his bed. At last he got it to work.

"Hey, Mom! Come here!"

[Satisfying conclusion]

See teacher directions, page 75.

Page 63: Spelling

Jonathon lay back on his bed and stared at the **knotted** pine boards above. David, his twin, **lounged** on the floor. The attic loft room, with the fan blowing across him, was the place to be on a warm summer day, Jonathon reflected, **especially** if none of the guys were around to play baseball or ride bikes. Pale blue walls reflected light from the window back into the room. The mulberry tree nearby **offered** shade from the heat of the day.

Lazily, Jonathon let his eyes roam over each of the boards, one by one. Suddenly he stopped.

"David, look! That board. It's **different**."

"Oh, it's just a knothole." David fiddled with the string in his hands.

Puzzled, Jonathon stared at the board. "It's shaped like a key. It even looks as if there's a **metal** plate around it, like a keyhole for a door."

"No," David said, "The wood's just darker there, or looks darker because of the hole. It's nothing out of the **ordinary**."

Jonathon kept looking at the hole. It certainly looked like a keyhole. "I wonder," he mused, "if I had a key and turned it in the keyhole, would a door or a **panel** open?" The only way to find out was to get a key and try it.

Jonathon sat up and swung his legs over the edge of the bed. He walked over to the desk and pulled the chair across the floor so that it was **positioned** directly under the hole.

Page 64: Capitalization

"Move, David." Standing on the chair, Jonathon reached up to feel the hole. **He** took his bike lock key out of his pocket and tried it in the keyhole.

"That doesn't come close to fitting," David protested.

Jonathon got off the chair and pushed it back over to the desk. "No," he said, "before I look for a key, I need to know what I'm looking for." He pushed the chair back over to the hole. Then he walked over to the desk, rummaged around, and found a piece of paper and a pencil.

"What are you doing?"

"You'll see." Jonathon climbed back up on the chair, holding the paper and pencil. **He** had to stand on tiptoe to reach the keyhole; even then, he had to reach up and lean his head back—it was most awkward, but he managed to get a key shape traced.

Answer Key *(cont.)*

"Now I'm ready to find the key!" In his enthusiasm, Jonathon forgot about the midday heat.

He ran down the stairs and banged out the screen door. **D**avid followed at a more leisurely pace and caught up with Jonathon on the porch.

"Where am I going to look first?" Staring out towards the mulberry tree, **J**onathon straddled the porch railing and pondered the best place to begin looking for a key. "I know! **I'**ll go down and check around the basement."

"**A**t least it's cool down there," David said.

See teacher directions, page 75.

Page 65: Punctuation

The two boys went around to the side of the **house**. The cool musty odor of the basement greeted Jonathan as he opened the door. He went down the narrow step **slowly**, allowing his eyes time to adjust to the darkness. Jonathon rounded the post at the bottom of the stairs and glanced at the shelves. He couldn't decide whether or not to search them thoroughly. Deciding not to, he turned around to survey the rest of the basement and almost bumped into David.

"It's too dark to look very well down here," Jonathon said. **"I'll** never find a key in this mess. If I did, it probably would be rusted and corroded and wouldn't **work."** He sighed and went up the stairs as slowly as he had gone down.

"Maybe the shop would be a good place to **look**," David suggested as they stepped around the corner into the backyard. The door to the shop was open, as usual, and Jonathon walked in. Now this, this was a fascinating place, even if it was messy.

"I've got to get serious about finding this key before **dinner**," Jonathon **said**. "After dinner, I want to play ball with the guys." Jonathon looked around as David stopped to fool with some tools on the workbench. Jonathon didn't see any keys on the workbench. He walked over to look at the pegboard, and sure enough, a key was hanging **there**. Jonathon looked at the key for a minute, studying it.

"It doesn't look like it fits the garage door, but I'll try it to be sure before I take it."

Page 66: Grammar

Discovering that the key **didn't** work in the garage door, he slipped it into the pocket of his jeans.

"Time to go see if this key works!" He jogged across the lawn and up the back porch. The screen door **banged** shut behind him.

"Wait for me!" David all of a sudden **burst** through the door and it slammed a second time.

Bounding the stairs two at a time, Jonathon turned on the landing and continued up the second flight of stairs. He **hesitated** when he got to his room, uncertain what would happen when he tried the key in the keyhole. The room looked the same as always, the chair just as he had left it, the shadows from the tree branches a little longer in the afternoon sun. Jonathon **took** the key out of his pocket and climbed up on the chair.

"Here goes." He tried the key in the hole. It went in halfway, then stopped.

"Let me try," David said. He took the key, turned it over, and tried again. It wouldn't begin to go in the keyhole this time.

Jonathon took a folded piece of paper out of his pocket.

Answer Key *(cont.)*

"Guess I should have checked the key shape against this tracing before I came back in the house. Now I have to start all over again looking for a key." He **sat** down on the edge of the bed, **rested** his chin in his hands, and stared out the window.

"I'm going outside," David said. "Come on, let's play catch."

See teacher directions, page 75.

Page 67: Paragraphs

"Okay. When we get together with the guys after dinner, I can ask them where else to look for an old key that would fit."

David had just tossed the ball to Jonathon when Michael sauntered by. "Hey, what'cha doing? Are we playing ball tonight?"

"Yeah, I guess so," Michael answered. "We're short a few, though. The Grays are out of town, and John has to go somewhere with his folks."

"Well," Jonathon said slowly, still not sure if he wanted to let anyone else help him discover what might lie behind the keyhole. "I know of something else we could do"

"What?"

Jonathon showed Michael the tracing of the key and tried to explain.

"Hmm, I don't know. I guess we can look for a key."

"Dinner!"

"We've got to go," Jonathon said. "Let's meet back here at 6:30 and we'll decide then what to do."

Thump, thump. Jonathon smacked the ball into his glove as he waited.

"Hi there. What's this I hear about a key?"

"Hi, Paul," Jonathon said. "I'll explain when everyone gets here."

Just then Michael walked up. "It looks like the only one we're waiting for now is Dan," he said.

Page 70: Corrected writing sample

This is my perfect planet. **M**y planet would be called Indefectibility. It would **have** 100 people**,** and all of my **friends would** be there**.**

I would also have **a variety** of animals. There would be lots of **skybats** and other dinosaurs. There would be mountain lions, lions, toads, frogs, insects, **mammals**, etc. The animals would have the same language as us.

The planet would have lots of plants, **but** it would not have any of the **poisonous** plants, like **poison** oak, **poison** ivy, stinging nettle, etc. All the plants would be **edible**. There would be forests.

The planet would also have no pollution and lots of rings and moons. There would be 7 moons and all of them would be different colors. There would be all the colors of the rainbow on the rings.

There would be good teachers **that** teach spelling, social studies, how to use the play equipment, etc. **T**hat would be my perfect planet, because that's what I like that doesn't always happen here. The planet would be bigger than **Jupiter**. **It would have** warm snow. That would be my perfect planet.

Technology Resources

Microsoft Publisher 97. Microsoft Corporation.

Desktop publishing program

The program enables students to incorporate original text with clip art to create their own publications.

Microsoft Word 97. Microsoft Corporation.

Desktop publishing program

Word also allows students to add clip art to their documents. It is easy to enter text and edit. The insert comment and auto correct features allow teachers to disable automatic corrections of common student errors and to edit and comment on student work.

Storybook Weaver Deluxe. MECC/The Learning Company (1994)

Writing program, ages 6–12

Pictures and sounds provide story starters for students to create their own stories. Stories may be written and edited within the program. Students may also hear their story read aloud back to them.

Student Writing Center. The Learning Company.

Desktop publishing program

Program includes five document types, writing process and grammar tips for students, and teacher's lesson ideas and worksheet templates.

Internet Web Sites

Merriam-Webster On-line: Dictionary

http://www.m-w.com/ netdict.htm
An easy-to-use dictionary that also offers a daily word game, a word of the day, and more.

Merriam-Webster On-line Thesaurus

http://www.m-w.com/thesaurus.htm
This is a top site that will do amazing synonym searches.

The Wordsmyth English Dictionary-Thesaurus

http://www.wordsmyth.net/
This is a basic, useful dictionary site.

Visual Thesaurus

http://plumbdesign.com/thesaurus/
This amazing site builds floating, 3D webs of word relationships. You will need a Java-capable browser in order to use it.

Word Dance

http://www.worddance.com/
Students can read samples of student-created stories, articles, and poetry at this online magazine. There are many other creative possibilities for word fun at this site.

Bibliography

Allard, Harry, and James Marshall. *Miss Nelson Is Missing.* Houghton Mifflin, 1977.

Banks, Lynne Reid. *The Indian in the Cupboard.* Avon Books, 1980.

Benson, Robert. *The Life of Prayer and the Art of Writing.* Retreat, 1998.

Bradby, Marie. *More Than Anything Else.* Orchard Books, 1995.

Cannon, Janell. *Stellaluna.* Scholastic, 1993.

Cleary, Beverly. *The Mouse and the Motorcycle.* William Morrow, 1965.

Coville, Bruce. *Jeremy Thatcher, Dragon Hatcher.* Pocket Books, Simon and Schuster, 1991.

Dahl, Roald. *Charlie and the Chocolate Factory.* Puffin Books, 1964.

Kline, Suzy. *Song Lee and the Leech Man.* Viking, 1995.

L'Engle, Madelaine. A *Wrinkle in Time.* Farrar, Strauss and Giroux, 1962.

Lester, Julius. *Sam and the Tigers.* Dial Books for Young Readers, 1996.

Lowry, Lois. *The Giver.* Bantam Doubleday Dell Books for Young Readers, 1993.

Morey, Walt. *Gentle Ben.* Avon Books, 1965.

Munsch, Robert. *David's Father.* Annick Press, 1983.

O'Dell, Scott. *Island of the Blue Dolphins.* Houghton Mifflin, 1960.

Paterson, Katherine. *Bridge to Terabithia.* Avon Books, 1977.

Paulsen, Gary. *Hatchet.* Aladdin Paperbacks. Simon and Schuster, 1987.

Paulsen, Gary. *The River.* Bantam Doubleday Dell Books, 1991.

Rowling, J.K. *Harry Potter and the Sorcerer's Stone.* Scholastic, 1997.

Sendak, Maurice. *Where the Wild Things Are.* HarperCollins, 1963.

Smith, Roland. *Thunder Cave.* Hyperion Books for Children, 1995.

Snyder, Zilpha K. *The Egypt Game.* Bantam Doubleday Dell Books, 1967.

Van Allsburg, Chris. *The Polar Express.* Houghton Mifflin, 1985.

Waber, Bernard. *Ira Sleeps Over.* Houghton Mifflin, 1972.

Woolbridge, Susan G. *poemcrazy*. Clarkson Potter, 1996.